KENNETH ROWNTREE

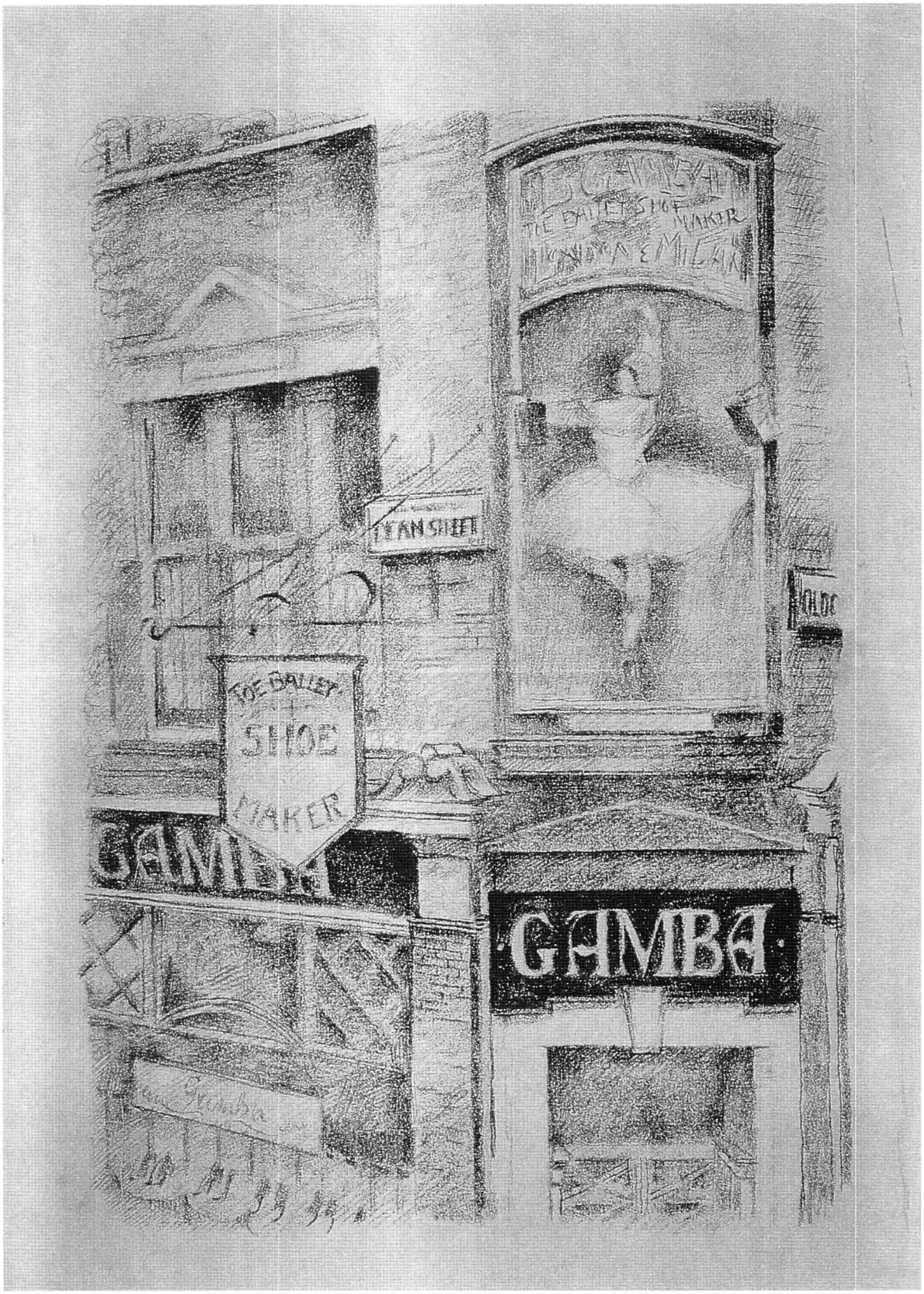
SHOE
MAKER
GAMBA

John Milner

With a chronology by Diana Rowntree

KENNETH ROWNTREE

Lund Humphries

First published in 2002 by
Lund Humphries
Gower House
Croft Road
Aldershot
Hampshire GU11 3HR

and

131 Main Street
Burlington
VT 05401
USA

www.lundhumphries.com

Lund Humphries is part of Ashgate Publishing

British Library Cataloguing-in-Publication Data
A catalogue record for this book is available from the British Library

ISBN 0 85331 850 6

Designed by Chrissie Charlton and Company
Typeset in Glypha by Tom Knott
Printed in Singapore under the supervision of MRM Graphics

Library of Congress / Control Number: 2001099519

Frontispiece:
Gamba Shoe Shop, Soho, London 1939
Lithograph on paper
28 x 20.4 cms (11 x 8 inches)

Contents

For Bonamy Devas

Acknowledgements

My first acknowledgement is to Diana Rowntree for her support in this project, always helpful and never seeking to influence its content. For her help and for her *Chronology* I am deeply grateful. Diana and her family made this book possible: my first thanks are to them and particularly to Adam Rowntree for his organisation of the archive and his answers to difficult questions. Since the completion of this manuscript the death of Esmond Devas means that he will not see the book about which he was unfailingly enthusiastic even during illness. Sasha, his widow, is also Kenneth Rowntree's daughter. For her I hope the optimism of his paintings offers irrepressible encouragement. I have dedicated the book to Bonamy Devas who carries an awareness of Kenneth Rowntree's art to a whole new generation.

Support from the Paul Mellon Foundation launched the work financially. Newcastle University paid for photographs skilfully prepared by the Audio-Visual Department, and there was support from Quaker charities to whom I am deeply grateful.

Dr Christopher Brown, Director of the Ashmolean Museum in Oxford and Dr Catherine Whistler of the Department of Western Art have shown faith in the project, as have Lucy Whetstone and Andrew Heard at the Hatton Gallery and Andrew Burton in the Department of Fine Art at Newcastle University. It is fitting that these three institutions play significant roles in its narrative. Other museums provided photographs, in particular the Victoria and Albert Museum, Imperial War Museum and Tate Gallery in London. Other paintings have been reproduced by permission of the National Library of Wales at Aberystwyth.

I am especially grateful to those individuals who allowed their works to be photographed and included in this book: Alan and Sarah Fearon, Mrs Humphrey Odd, and Mrs Gordon Ryder, and all those who chose anonymity, as well as many enthusiastic owners of works by Rowntree, including Percy and Mary Lovell. I am pleased to acknowledge also the enthusiastic support and help of the Fry Public Art Gallery, Saffron Walden, Essex. Thank you, too, Angela Horn and Beryl Carnaffin for essential help at the last moment.

A final accolade must go to the Liddicott sisters for their devoted preservation and recent revelation of an early master work.

I Early Days

Kenneth Rowntree's life stretched from World War I to the final decade of the twentieth century. He vividly reflected the times in which he lived and its opportunities. But two circumstances above all affected his outlook from the beginning: he was a Quaker and a Yorkshireman.

Rowntree, the painter, constantly revised his techniques, but he pursued subjects for many years, picking up a motif after sixty years as if he had never left it. He was equally aware of developments in art and of his appetite for the world he saw around him through his circular lenses (Fig.1).

Rowntree was not an isolated artist: he was convivial. He was a pacifist whose work was acquired by the Wartime Artists Advisory Committee. He had contacts and friendships of international range and ambitions which led him to France, Italy, America and Australia, but he chose to be defined, too, by his sense of place and by close observation of familiar and ordinary life in the particular places where he lived.

Kenneth Rowntree was born in Scarborough on 14 March 1915. His parents, Howard and Nora Rowntree, were both from Quaker families. An undated pamphlet, published in Nottingham and found in Rowntree's papers, depicts a Quaker in a wide-brimmed hat and buckled shoes to illustrate the *Anecdotes of the Quakers, instructive and amusing, of their Shrewdness, Wit, Disinterestedness, Benevolence and Moral Heroism.*[1] Some of these qualities Rowntree had in abundance. He embraced Quaker pacifism; he was surprising, independent and verbally astute and had confidence in his own judgement.

His father managed the family department store and Rowntree's earliest works were displayed there. His mother trained as a violinist at the

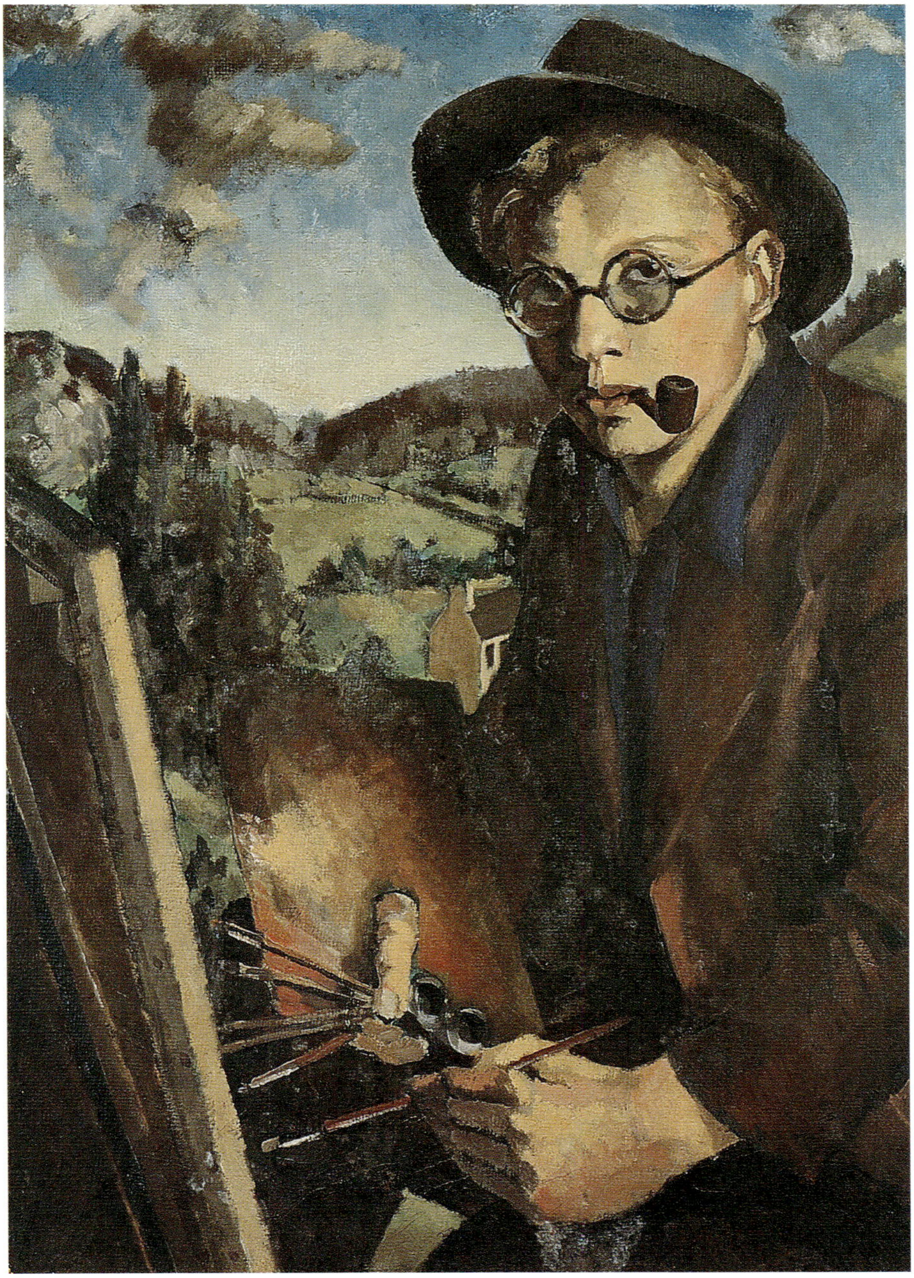

1 Early Self-Portrait, Levisham 1933
Oil on canvas
91.5 x 70.1 cms (36 x 28 inches)

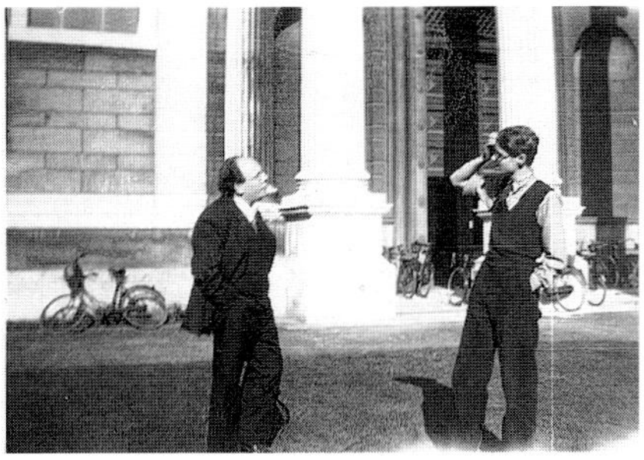

2 Kenneth Rowntree (right)
with the painter Barnett Freedman outside
the Ashmolean Museum, Oxford *c.*1934
Photograph

Royal College of Music. Kenneth Rowntree, too, studied the cello in his school days and music recurs as a theme in his works. Painting, however, was stronger and was further encouraged by Maurice Feild, his art master at the Downs School, Herefordshire, where he first met Lawrence Gowing, later to become a distinguished painter, art historian and lifelong friend. From 1929 to 1932, Rowntree attended Bootham Quaker School in York.

In 1932, aged eighteen, Rowntree enrolled at the Ruskin Drawing School in Oxford. A photograph shows him with his friend Douglas Pittock, walking along St Giles in Oxford, with his coat flung over his shoulder; another shows him in lively debate with his tutor, the painter Barnett Freedman.[2] The photograph illustrates a setting for study, argument, social contact, architecture and high art.

The challenge Oxford presented might have overwhelmed Rowntree but for the support of the painter Albert Rutherston, Ruskin Master and Principal of the School since 1929. His teaching was informal, operating from Monday to Wednesday and from 10 am to 4 pm before moving to the Randolph Hotel for refreshments. Rutherston had been exhibiting in London at the Leicester Galleries since 1926. By the time Rutherston showed there in 1934, Rowntree was a prize pupil, winner of the 1933 Life Drawing Prize and the 1934 Life Painting Prize.

Rutherston, who anglicised his name from Rothenstein, had Yorkshire connections and was the brother of John Rothenstein, soon to become Director of the Tate Gallery and also a family friend of the Rowntrees. From the summer of 1920 Albert had worked in the Oxford Life School, taken over by Ruskin in 1922, and where Paul Nash was an occasional visiting tutor. For Rowntree, Rutherston was a link to a wider world, with work on show, not only at at the Oxford Arts Club (November–December 1934) and the Leicester Galleries, but also at the New English Art Club and at the Royal Watercolour Society in London.[3] Rutherston also acquired Rowntree's *Guitar Players*, an oil painting of 1933 that he valued enough to bequeath to the Tate Gallery.[4]

From the Ruskin School, Rowntree moved to the Slade School, London, where his tutors included the painter Randolph Schwabe. He did not take well to the transition. His rooms in Windmill Street were less than a mile away, but he remained independent, preferring his own pace and ideas to the demands of the famous art school. He expanded his horizons by spending time in museums and galleries, and he began to paint in France, drawing in the Luxembourg Gardens in Paris in 1935, and returning there over the next few years.

Numerous artists teaching at the Slade School maintained a close interest in French painting, and a small *Life Study* (Fig.3), painted by Rowntree in 1936, reflects this tradition. The pose and cool colours reflect an awareness of Degas and Sickert nudes. The warmer areas of subdued yellow reveal the colour of the board beneath the paint. Rowntree has adopted the French device of moving the model from the life room into a more domestic interior with all the potential for reportage, scrutiny and narrative that it might entail. Here Rowntree has achieved a sense of stillness, space and light. The love of blue, the featureless face, the sense of an inhabited interior – all of these will be seen throughout his work.

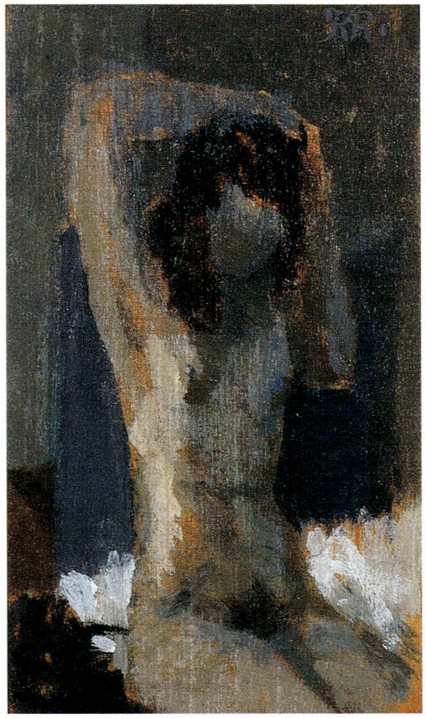

3 Life Study *c.*1936
Oil on board
19.1 x 11.4 cms (7.5 x 4.5 inches)

A spectacular celebration followed in Rowntree's first large painting, the triptych *Homage to French Culture in the Nineteenth Century* of 1938 (Fig.4). This colourful and monumental tribute to French painting, literature, music and landscape was painted on three panels used as a folding screen. It catalogues Rowntree's every French enthusiasm. It was commissioned by Mr and Mrs J. R. Liddicott who saw an advertisement placed in the family store of W. H. Rowntree & Sons in Scarborough.[5]

The central tableau displays the attributes of painting (palette), literature (pen) and music (score). The painter Cézanne is served a drink at right, and Degas' face is framed by the distant vista of Paris. Magically, the Normandy coast appears top centre with cornfields, villages and mountains to the left. Every figure is identifiable, from Rousseau to Cézanne, and above them all, Apollo's crown of laurel is awarded to the whole of nineteenth-century French culture by an angelic figure in white. Beneath her in the foreground a young girl, derived from Degas' *Bellelli Family* portrait, presents her flowers. A magnificent testament to Rowntree's erudition and delight in French culture, this first large composition is constructed from multiple elements, a kind of catalogue of parts, building up the message of the whole.

Stylistically, it is characterised by a deliberate suggestion of primitive technique, offering the viewer a puzzling mixture of sophistication and witty naïveté, derived in itself from French painters such as Le Douanier Rousseau, from stylised decorative motifs (as in the white flying figure borrowed from the great French muralist Puvis de Chavannes) to a

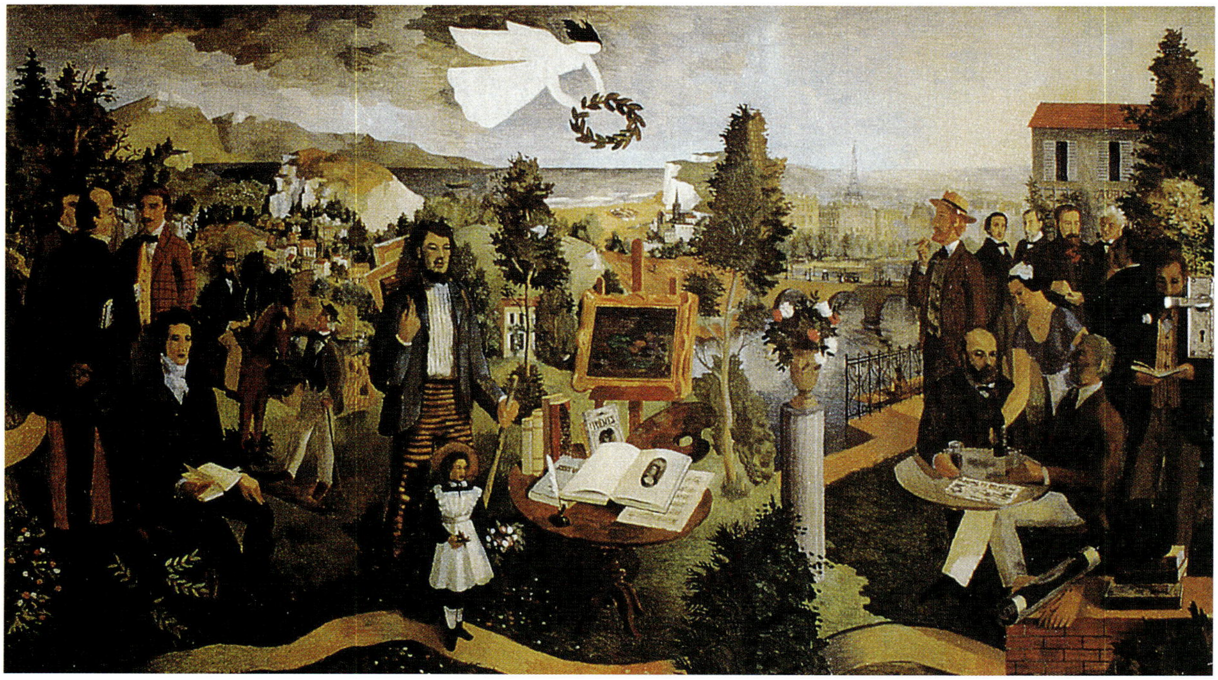

4 Homage to French Culture in the Nineteenth Century 1938
Oil on wood
132 x 236 cms (52 x 93 inches)
Collection The Daughters of Jack and Yvonne Liddicott, Scarborough

deliberate dislocation of space (the surprising developments of the landscape background) and of scale (the smallness of the foreground girl). Rowntree had the ability and confidence to comment with visual wit on the work of others, to sustain an appetite for art of many kinds, and to make approachable, enjoyable paintings that remain instinctive and original.

This synthesis of French culture within a commission in Scarborough reflects both Rowntree's new horizons and his background. A small study of a *Waitress* (Fig.5) recalls French bar scenes and even, perhaps, a Yorkshireman's impression of Manet's *Bar at the Folies-Bergère*. The deep browns are foreign to Manet's canvas but there are wine bottles here on the shelves and a figure reflected in the mirror. By contrast, a pint of stout stands on the counter. The slight stiffness of the waitress calculating the bill recalls the triptych's figures, and an early *Still-Life at Furlongs* has similar qualities, an interior with a strong personality redolent of the people that used it. The pre-war works showed many other French devices and he continued to visit France, making paintings of Gisors, Normandy, in 1936, 1938 and 1939.[6]

Kenneth Rowntree's first self-portrait (Fig.1), painted in 1933, conjures up a Yorkshire valley with a house (visible behind the palette). The eighteen-year-old painter looks frankly at his image, the characteristic

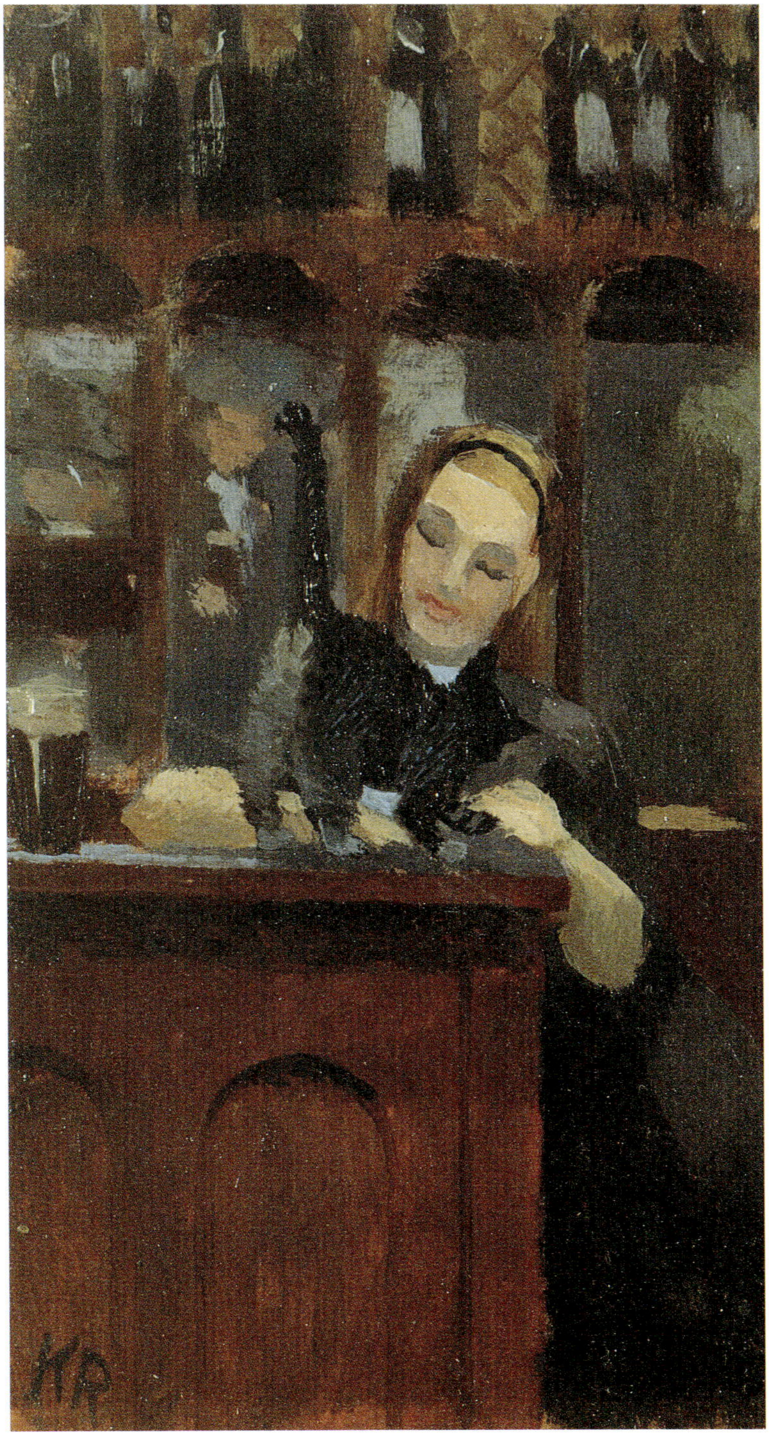

5 Waitress
Oil on canvas
Size and whereabouts unknown

spectacles already in place, yet there is little sense of introspection. This is a confident assertion of commitment and background, the image of a real professional, reliably mature with pipe and hat, though a dynamic youth nevertheless. It is almost a shop sign, a dramatic example of his skill, inviting the viewer to meet the painter.

By the late 1930s Rowntree was independent but still careful to maintain Yorkshire connections. He had also grown close to Diana Buckley, who had joined the first year class in architecture at the Ruskin School in 1934. Their holiday in Sweden in September 1938 was reflected in a still-life (Fig.6) which is a kind of double portrait by association. On a table elevated above the shore lie their bathing costumes, a powerful evocation of the personalities that had recently occupied them, extended further by Diana's bathing hat, Kenneth's spectacles and pipe, and their wine bottle and books. The picture is in fact a narrative, involving the bathers' departure and the imminent arrival of a small boat (seen to the left). In the distance, sailing boats move across the skyline.

The emotional tension of this narrative recalls the political events of 1938, with Europe on the edge of war. In a collage of 1938 Rowntree celebrated the Munich agreement that seemed to hold out a last hope of peace. Here the dove of peace delivers her olive branch to the newspapers of Italy, Russia, Switzerland, Germany and France. Kenneth Rowntree's Quaker background is evident in this poetic evocation of pacifism. He has adopted the pasted newspaper technique of cubist collages and Picasso's doves. The *Holiday in Sweden*, too, was basically cubist in structure. Picasso, Braque and Juan Gris had frequently linked still-life and landscape in this way in the 1920s and into the 1930s. Picasso especially used its ambiguous picture space as a setting for disturbingly animated objects. Since the 1936 *International Surrealist Exhibition* in London, such animated objects had become familiar in painting.[7] The *Swedish Still-Life* is, of course, a celebration, but these clothes reflect the personality of their owners, lending them a kind of vitality not unlike the animated objects of Surrealism.

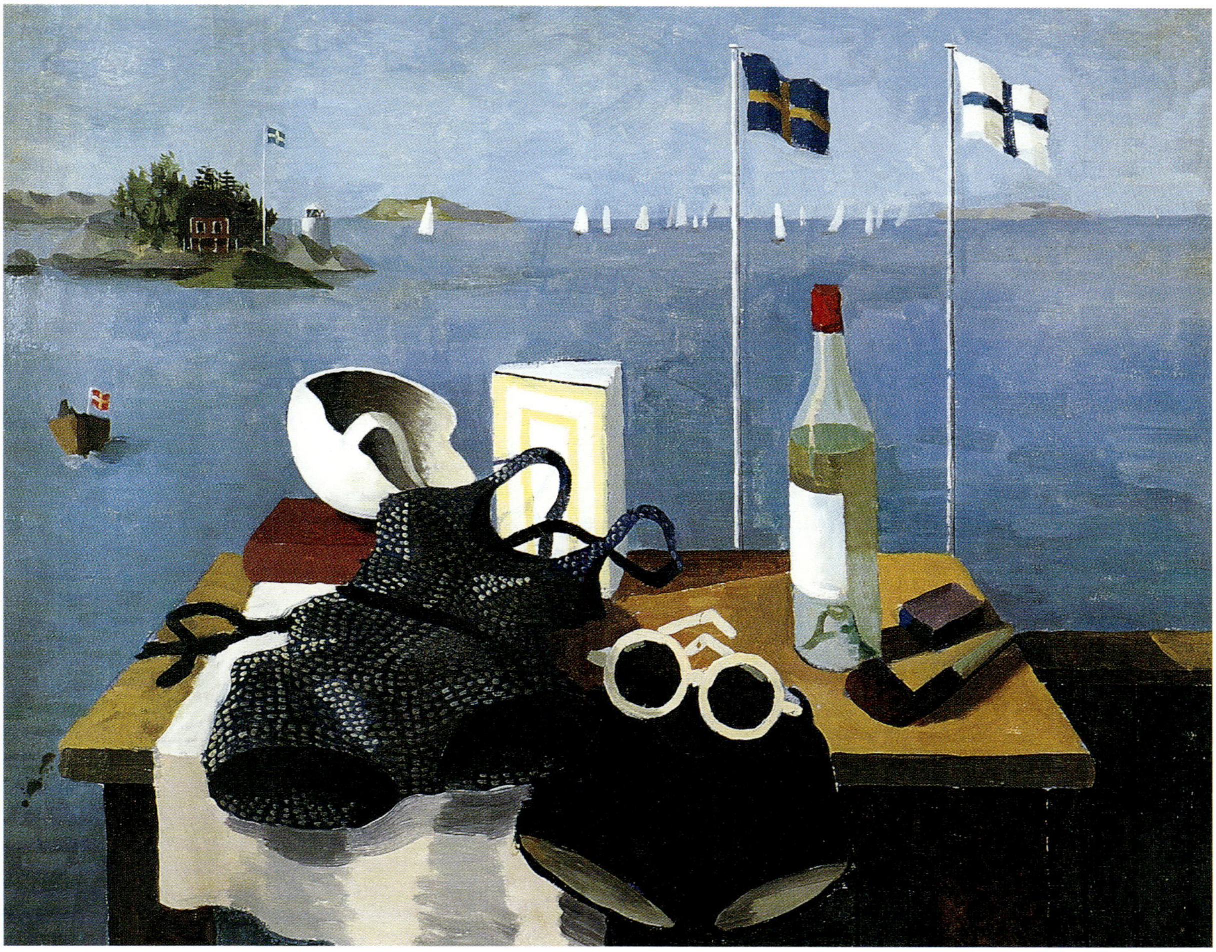

6 Holiday in Sweden 1938
Oil on canvas
50.8 x 69.7 cms (20 x 27.5 inches)
Collection John and Lesley Milner

II War

War was so likely that on 29 August 1939 Kenneth Clark, Director of the National Gallery, proposed setting up an advisory committee on the employment of artists in wartime.[8] Clark's contact was the painter E. M. O'Rourke Dickey, now a civil servant but before 1931 Professor of Fine Art in Durham University at Newcastle.[9]

War was declared against Germany on 3 September 1939. Kenneth Rowntree and Diana Buckley married five days later. Diana had by now qualified as an architect from the Architectural Association's School of Architecture in London. Her architectural concerns were to have a profound effect on Kenneth's art. A small wedding party was held at Lawn Road Flats, Hampstead, the pioneering building of 1934 by Wells Coates. The structure was a British response to the continental architecture of Le Corbusier, Gropius and others. These apartments were undemanding, efficient, ingenious and simple. The flat roof was a communal space and there was a restaurant run by Philip Harben. Jack Pritchard, a prime mover in the Lawn Road project, became a lifelong friend. He progressed from being an importer of plywood to become a vital link for refugee artists and designers fleeing Europe in the late 1930s.[10] He knew Bauhaus staff including its former director and founder, Walter Gropius, and the painter-designer Laszlo Moholy-Nagy who had worked on the Basic Course at the Bauhaus. These men had many other contacts. They were at the centre of the great exodus from war-torn, Nazi-dominated Europe that carried ideas to Britain and from there to the United States, transforming art, architecture and design in the process. It was a principle of Bauhaus teaching that artists and technicians should come together under the discipline of architecture to reshape society.

Given its emphasis on design and lifestyle this was by no means an obvious environment for Kenneth Rowntree's approach to painting with

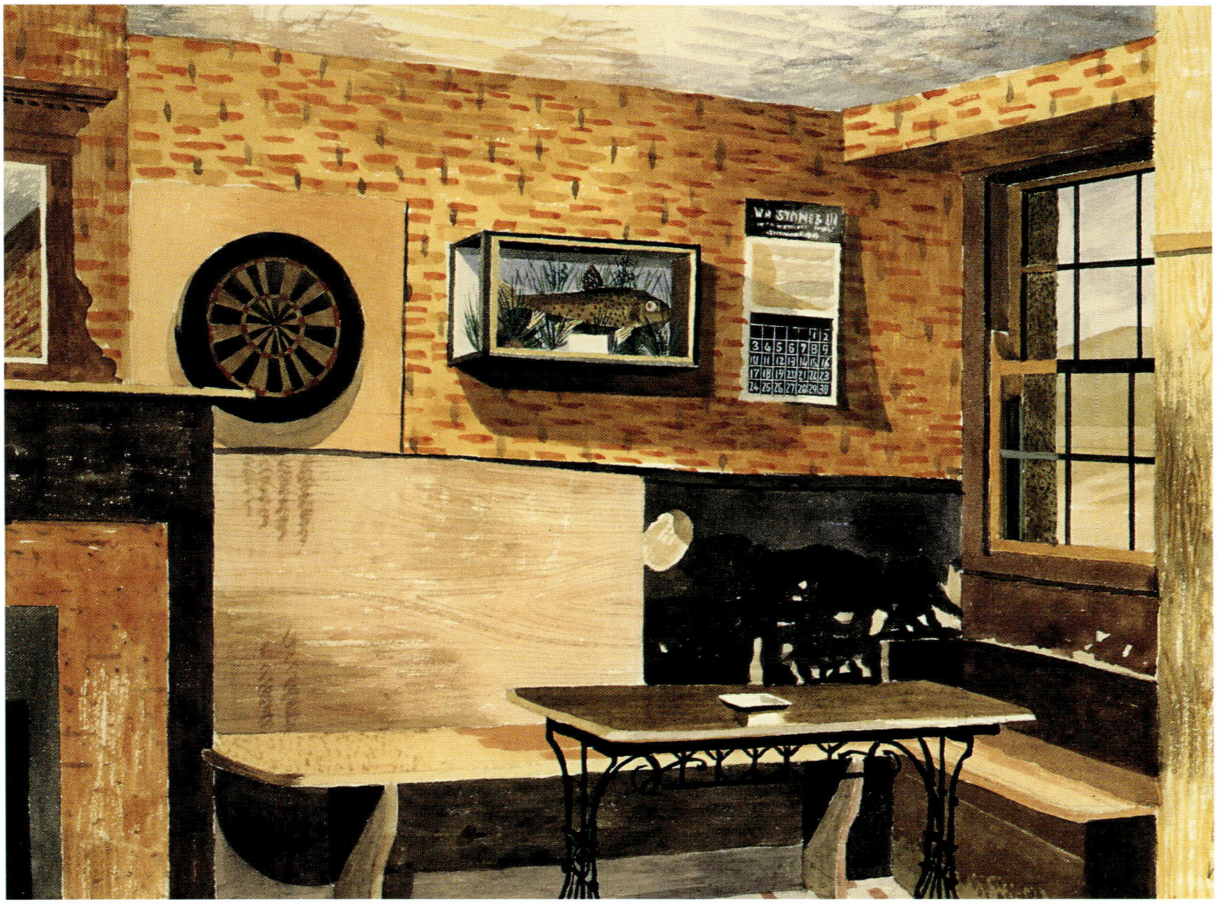

7 The Smoke Room, Ashopton Inn, Ashopton, Derbyshire 1940
Watercolour heightened with chinese white on paper
Signed and dated in pencil *Kenneth Rowntree '40*
32.4 x 49.5 cms (12.75 x 19.5 inches)
Board of Trustees of the Victoria and Albert Museum, London (E.1265-1949)

its strong sense of place and observation, but he had married an adventurous architect, contemporary in her interests and intelligent in her analysis of the function of design in architecture. After a holiday at Clare in Suffolk, where Kenneth was often to paint,[11] they moved into Lawn Road Flats. Diana recalled that 'we found the concrete world as stimulating as we had imagined (and drawn) it.'[12]

Recording Britain

But war would make London increasingly dangerous and air raids were expected immediately. On 3 October 1939 Kenneth Clark wrote to the Ministry of Labour, 'I need not tell you what terrible distress the war is causing among artists .... The situation is so serious that I have been wondering if it would not be desirable for the Government to take some action .... I have in mind something like the federal scheme for artists carried out in America during the last five years or so, though ours would no doubt have to be on a less ambitious scale ... it would have a wonderful effect on English art in general.'[13]

A scheme was approved on 7 November 1939 with the first meeting of the Wartime Artists Advisory Committee (WAAC) two weeks later. The armed services and major London art schools were represented, with Schwabe representing the Slade. At the weekly meetings commissions and purchases were made, ranging in value from a maximum of £10 for a watercolour to £300 for a large oil painting. There was no explicit demand for propaganda.

As a Quaker, it was vital for Rowntree to find a role in the war compatible with his pacifism. It must have been a relief when Clark commissioned Rowntree to produce work for the WAAC late in 1939.[14] Artists were to 'make drawings, painting and prints at the war front, in factories, workshops, shipyards and on the land, and of the changed life of the towns and villages, thus making a permanent record of life during the war which would be a memorial to the national effort, and of particular value.'[15] The home front aspect of this project effectively included the scheme known as Recording Britain, to which Rowntree contributed large watercolours made in Yorkshire, Derbyshire, Essex and Wales.[16] Their inventiveness and originality arose in part from his inexperience in watercolour: unfamiliar with its conventions, he devised innovative techniques.[17]

The Pilgrim Trust, a charity set up by Edward Stephen Harkness of New York in 1930 to meet urgent British needs in terms of social welfare, art and learning, supported the establishment of Recording Britain, paying artists about £5 for each watercolour accepted. Clark wanted paintings of ancient landscapes likely to be spoiled by housing developments and industry, records of towns and villages with old buildings about to be pulled down, parish churches which 'will fall down unless ruined by restoration', as well as country houses and parks.[18] Clark was worried as much by developers as by German invasion.

Rowntree chose Ashopton and Derwent, villages in Derbyshire soon to be engulfed by the Ladybower Reservoir, a good example of the threat posed by new developments rather than warfare, as the pub would soon be a hundred feet below water. *The Smoke Room* (Fig.7) shows a lost place. Rowntree's interior itemises each characteristic detail of wallpaper, benches, dartboard and torn black seating. The gloomy interior is deserted in a premonition of its ghostly future; the stuffed fish in its case will be returned to its natural element. Rowntree is describing the loss of a way of life here, as Recording Britain paid him to do. Recording Britain revealed a whole new aspect of his art, part topographical, part architectural, and part shrewd sociological observation of what buildings and decorations say about people. His paintings were enjoyable because they were recognisably full of local experience. They were also a lament for a vanishing Britain and this emphasised an historical dimension to his work, a geology, including architectural monuments and the lifestyle of the 1940s.[19] In *Underbank Farm, Woodlands, Ashdale, Derbyshire* (Fig.8), the hillside shows older lines diagonally crossing the walls and furrows that dominate his view, suggesting earlier farms.[20] The farmhouse and enclosures are prim and neat, facing the viewer like portraits of their inhabitants with much to say of their income, achievements and way of life. The painting links past and present with a future that is now our present, since the village and farm have vanished.[21]

The frontal view became a regular device for Rowntree combining all the qualities of architectural elevation, full of factual information, detail and texture, like a communal portrait to be scrutinised for expression. In his *Wesleyan Methodist Chapel at Ashopton* distant space is denied by the chapel's close fit within the rectangle of the painting. Windows stare back like eyes. The detail of lettering on a plaque, *Wesleyan Methodist Chapel 1840*, is complete down to the flourish of decorative motifs at its corners. The net curtains are a screen of dots that make a patterned

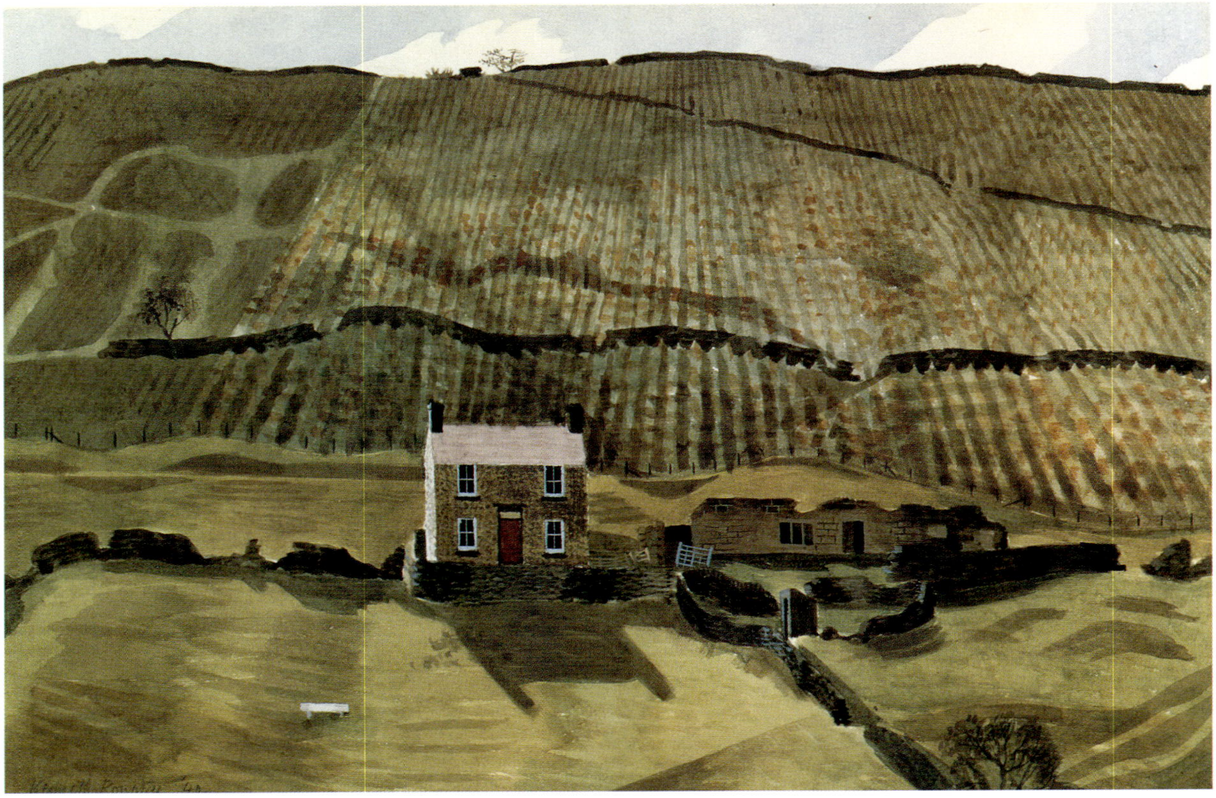

8 Underbank Farm, Woodlands, Ashdale, Derbyshire 1940
Watercolour on paper
Signed and dated in pencil *Kenneth Rowntree '40*
31.7 x 49cms (12.5 x 19.25 inches)
Board of Trustees of the Victoria and Albert Museum, London (E.1259-1949)

9 Foreign Servicemen in Hyde Park:
Early Summer 1940
Oil on canvas
45.7 x 76.2 cms (18 x 30 inches)
The Imperial War Museum, London
(IMW:ART LD 415)

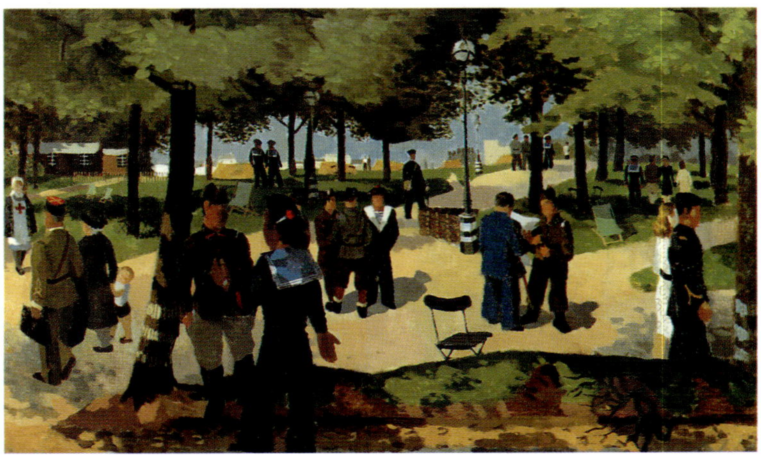

texture, as do the stone blocks, the roof slates, the railings and the open gates with curled uprights. These details provoke a careful, pleasurable scrutiny, a sense of knowing this individual place.

These watercolours met the aims of Recording Britain but did not reflect warfare. But the Wartime Artists Advisory Committee also commissioned from Rowntree oil paintings, now in the Imperial War Museum, London. Their size, the solidity of their dense bright colour, and a preference for social themes populated by many figures, make them a contrast to Recording Britain. These paintings could help the population at home to recognise changes in their life and identity. By contrast, other artists' skyscapes of fighter planes or landscapes with fighting tanks might seem alien and less credible images.

Rowntree's *Foreign Servicemen in Hyde Park: Early Summer 1940* (Fig.9) is a colourful reworking of Manet's *Music in the Tuileries Gardens*: even the folding chairs look French. Yet Bayswater is visible in the distance and this is clearly wartime. There is a Red Cross nurse at the left, a French officer before her, French sailors walking and signs of courtship in the dappled sunlight. This intensely fresh painting is a convivial image of wartime London, full of incidental optimism for the forces and nations meeting on the divergent paths of Hyde Park.

Late in the summer of 1940 Kenneth Rowntree painted *A Polo Ground in Wartime 1940* (Fig.10) for the WAAC. Late sun casts long shadows from ochre-yellow tents and mounds of earth. The alternative title, *Wartime Allotments, Ranelagh*, indicates that this polo field in Battersea Park had been requisitioned for allotments in which soldiers are planting vegetables. The pavilion and the sunlit scoreboard stand redundant in the evening light. A man with bucket, spade and pickaxe comes through the open gate; further back a woman in white and red walks towards the viewer with a young child. In this minutely detailed painting numerous soldiers in shirtsleeves tend their garden patches and, left of centre, there is a small but convincing image of a young woman in white riding away on a bicycle. The foreground is bathed in the cool shadow of a tree. The day's effort is ending in a blaze of sun but the familiar park is changed by war. The fading sunlight picks out the barrage balloons (left) that wait for night-time air raids. This kind of painting is colourful and pleasurable, but it is also social painting with changing lifestyle as its subject. But London was not so welcoming when bombs began to fall. When Diana was pregnant in 1941, a move was imperative. Friends and Recording Britain made it possible.

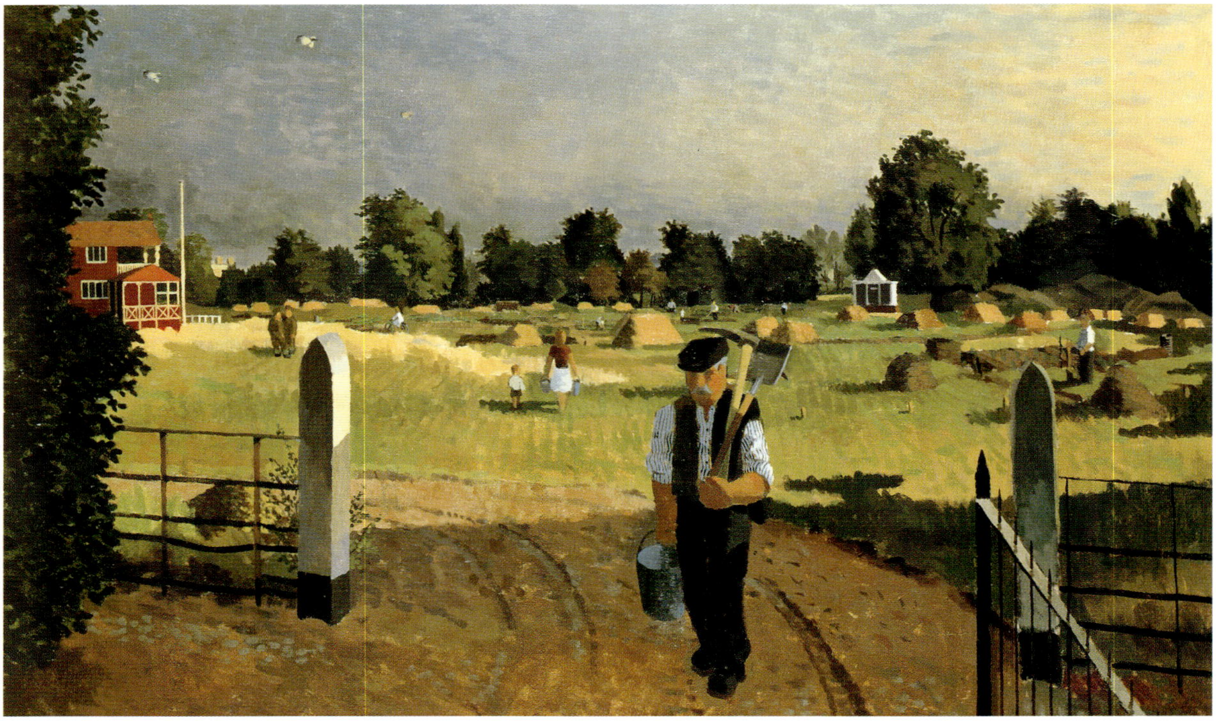

10 A Polo Ground in War-time 1940
(also known as *War-time Allotments, Ranelagh*)
Oil on canvas
55.8 x 91.4 cms (22 x 36 inches)
The Imperial War Museum, London (IMW:ART LD 637)

Eric Ravilious and his wife Thirzah found a house for the Rowntrees at Great Bardfield in Essex. Kenneth Rowntree painted a double portrait of them in 1941.[22] The area was almost an artists' colony. Eric and Thirzah Ravilious lived nearby at Shalford and Edward Bawden's house was almost next door, though Bawden was away on war service.

In painting parts of Essex for Recording Britain, Rowntree focused chiefly on church architecture. His watercolour of *St Peter and St Paul, Little Saling in Essex* has its great round tower rising from meadow grasses, a memorable image of the East Anglian summer but painted after careful thought and with attention to historical detail.
The viewpoint is low and the grass is high; wax has been drawn onto the textured paper to resist the watercolour so that feathery effects can be achieved. The detail includes structural elements of the church, its buttresses, the mouldings of medieval windows, stone quoins and weathering where the flint pebble construction is revealed. Rowntree depicted buildings as condensers of the history, nature and identity of places.

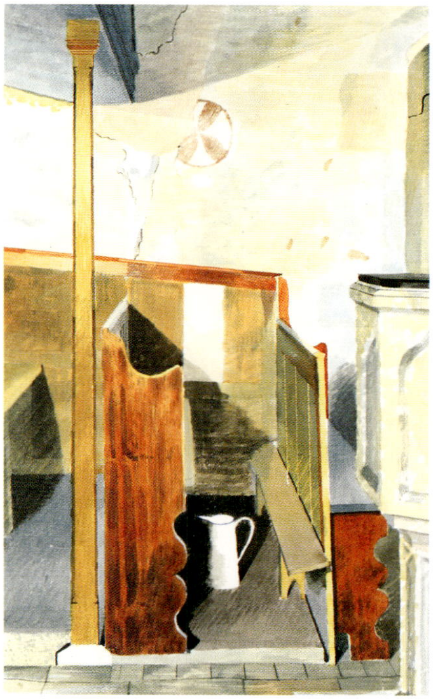

11 Interior, Church of Saints Peter and Paul, Little Saling, Essex *c.*1941
Watercolour on paper.
Signed in pencil lower left *Kenneth Rowntree*
48.2 x 29.3 cms (19 x 11.7 inches)
Board of Trustees of the Victoria and Albert Museum, London (E.1412-1949)

The interior view of the church (Fig.11) is an intimate and fragmentary view of the Elizabethan stone pulpit, wooden pews and cracked plaster. Rhythmic repetitions structure his painting: the pulpit arch, the wooden boards (again marked out with wax), the double-s curve of the pulpit edge where it meets the floor – these make for an elaborate composition. The enamel jug is for watering flowers no longer visible, a trace of the women who decorate this space to keep it fragrant and a place apart. The objects stand for people through their various functions and purposes. They spell out the life here.

In *The Livermore Gravestones, Barnston, near Dunmow, Essex* (Fig.12), the tombstones literally spell out the people they commemorate. Rowntree has observed every detail of the inscriptions to Martha Susannah (*d.* 1827), Emma (*d.* 1840), Jane (*d.* 1841) and Maria (*d.* 1841). They all died young and this elegy in a country churchyard presents the facts plainly, each on its sentinel stone in front elevation. Trees rise behind a wooden fence, every plank of which is carefully delineated.[23]

Rowntree's love of lettering may have been triggered by Ravilious at Oxford or refreshed by contact with him in Essex. Church interiors provided him with a rich range of alphabets, undisturbed and sheltered from the weather. *Interior, Black Chapel, North End, Essex* depicts skewed woodwork with meticulous attention to its idiosyncrasies,

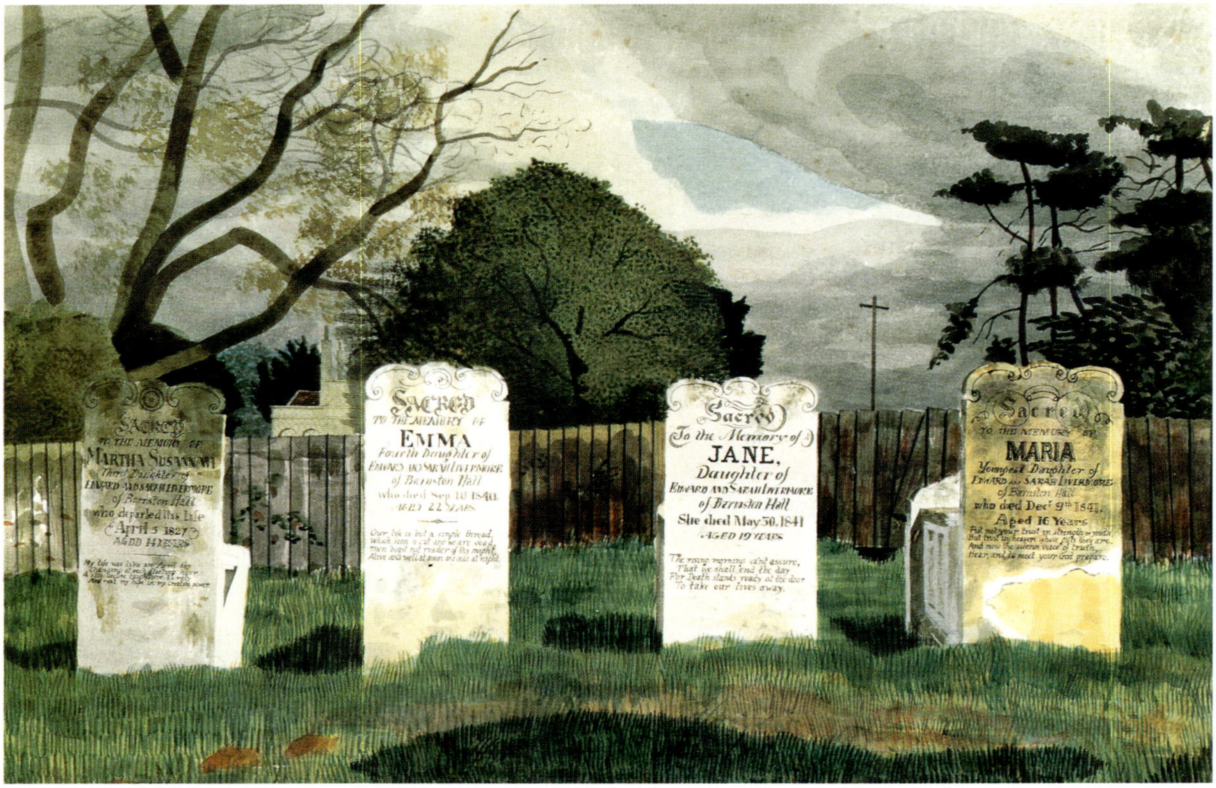

12 The Livermore Gravestones, Barnston, near Dunmow, Essex *c.*1941
Watercolour on paper
Signed in pencil *Kenneth Rowntree*
31.9 x 48 cms (12.5 x 18.9 inches)
Board of Trustees of the Victoria and Albert Museum, London (E.1407-1949)

equal to that applied to lettering on the black boards behind the altar proclaiming 'The Lord's Prayer', 'The Ten Commandments' and 'The Creed'.[24] The lack of people in these church interiors supports the effect of objects standing in for them, but also evokes an effect of silence (Fig.13).

Sometimes, the architecture Rowntree recorded was grandiose, as it had been in *The Priory Church at Dunstable* and in Yorkshire at *Guisborough Priory* and *Rievaulx Abbey*, or it could be mundane. *The House at Easingwold, Yorkshire* (Fig.14) is ordinary enough. As usual the front elevation dominates, with windows upstairs, a shop display at street level and an arch through to the back. The shop sells clothes, which enliven this deserted scene with evidence of human forms – at left, a ghostly image of mother and daughter, stockings or boots; in the centre, festive dresses and ribboned hats encased in the glass, while the right window displays rural Yorkshire respectability in nine shirts, four hats and four ties.[25]

These objects represent people. They look as lively as images of real people. One watercolour for Recording Britain shows *A Doll, representing an orphan, in a Northampton vestry* (Fig.15).

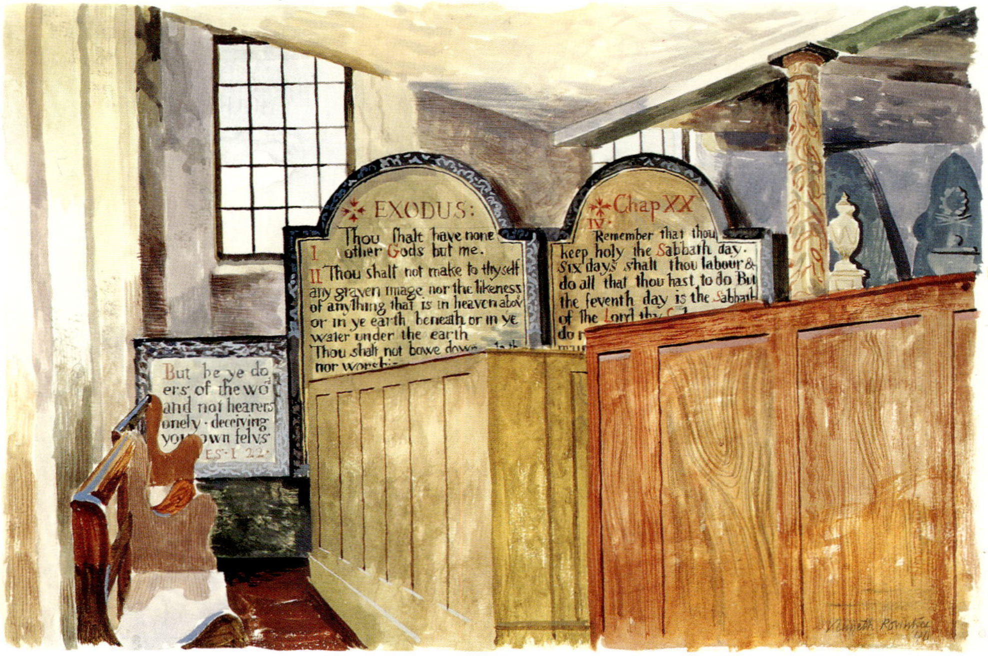

13 Pews in St Mary's Church, Whitby 1940
Watercolour on paper; Signed and dated in pencil *Kenneth Rowntree '40*
31.5 x 47 cms (12.5 x 18.5 inches)
Board of Trustees of the Victoria and Albert Museum, London (E.2592-1949)

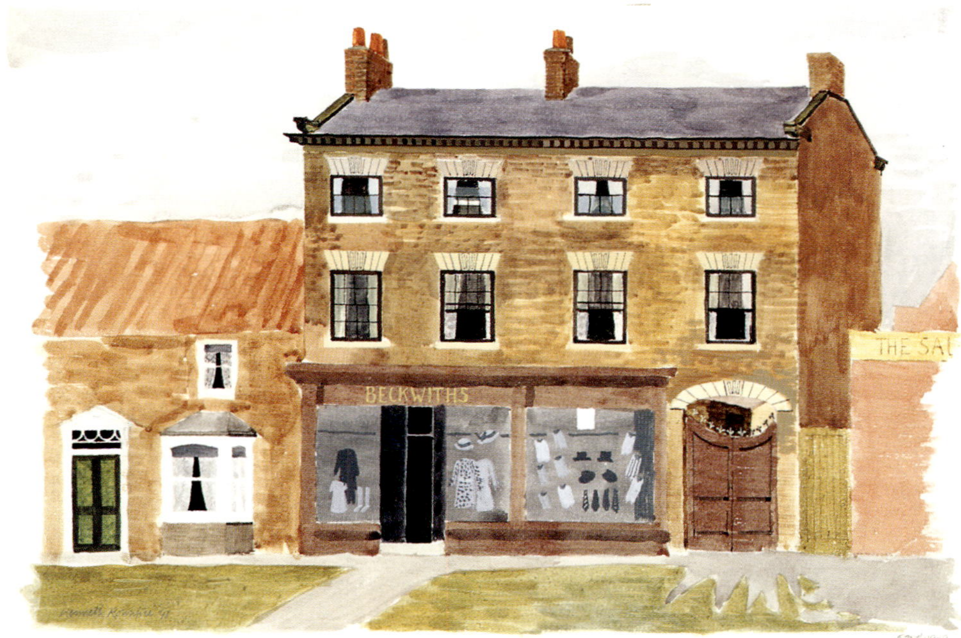

14 The House at Easingwold, Yorkshire 1940
Watercolour and body colour on paper
Signed and dated in pencil *Kenneth Rowntree '40*
31.5 x 49 cms (12.5 x 19.25 inches)
Board of Trustees of the Victoria and Albert Museum, London (E.2576-1949)

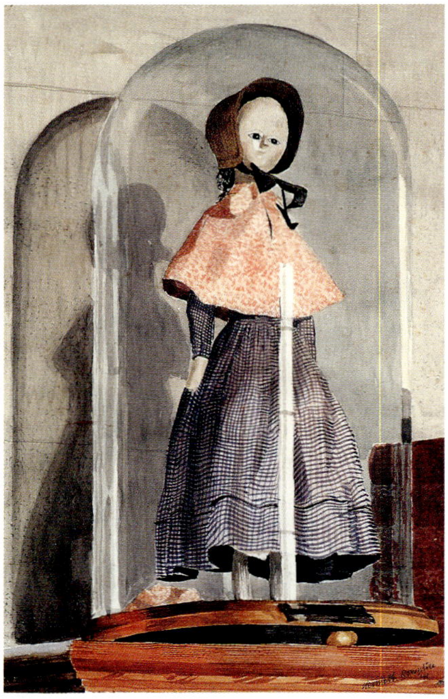

15 A Doll, representing an orphan, in a Northampton vestry *c.*1941
Watercolour on paper
48 x 32 cms (19 x 12.5 inches)

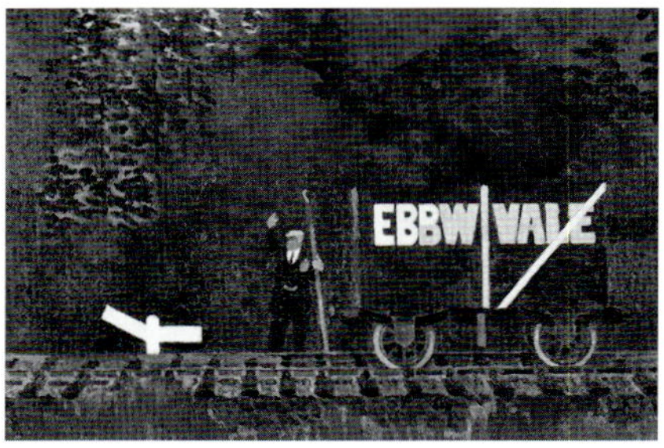

16 The Shunter (Ebbw Vale) 1943
Oil on canvas
25.5 x 39.5 cms (10 x 15.5 inches)
Formerly Collection Sally Race

Stylised figures of dolls, puppets and toys have a strange vitality in painting. The dramatic and disquieting effect achieved suggests narratives from another time.[26]

East Anglia fascinated Rowntree, but Rowntree had also loved Wales since spending holidays there as a boy. Social comment again began to emerge from topographic paintings. The most magnificent was *Conway Castle and Coracle, Caernarvonshire* (Fig.17) in which massive medieval towers against a mottled sky compete with foreground sheds and a railway sign *L.M.S.* The Welsh coracle, more intriguing than all the other structures, dominates the foreground. He records the great castle, but also daily life of his own time, bringing together the past and present as tourism does, and as posters increasingly illustrated.

Country cottages in the Conway Valley seems timeless by contrast: the elevation is carefully delineated like a new variation on an old theme, a little different in every region, here with stone walls, and the corrugated roofing of Welsh chapels.[27]

On the other hand, Welsh oil paintings of 1943 introduce themes of industrialisation, slate mines and railways, a mechanised world in which the human figure is central. In *The Shunter (Ebbw Vale)* (Fig.16) a railway freight truck presents its side elevation. At left, a railway post indicates an incline which the railwayman unconsciously echoes in his own raised arm. He stands square and practical by the railway line in a suit with waistcoat and watch-chain. In his tie and flat hat he is perhaps an engineer ensuring that coal moves from Ebbw Vale, a theme hard to reconcile with the aims of depicting vanishing aspects of British life and landscape as Recording Britain required.

Oil paintings for the WAAC examined daily life in wartime London on a larger scale. *CEMA Canteen Concert, Isle of Dogs, London E14* (Fig.18)[28] is an intricate canvas in which areas of colour are painted separately, as Paul Nash would paint them: there is no mixing of colour on the surface. The painting contains at least forty figures and a mass of patterning from decorated plates, stripes on shirts and hats and clothes, characterising people at the works canteen concert. The blue spot skirt in the foreground, the kerchief on the table, the rhythm of flat hats and windows evoke an atmosphere of expectation. As the announcer proclaims his words from the little stage, a young woman with a cello inches out from the shadows of the door to play for the men before they return to their war effort in the factory visible through the window.

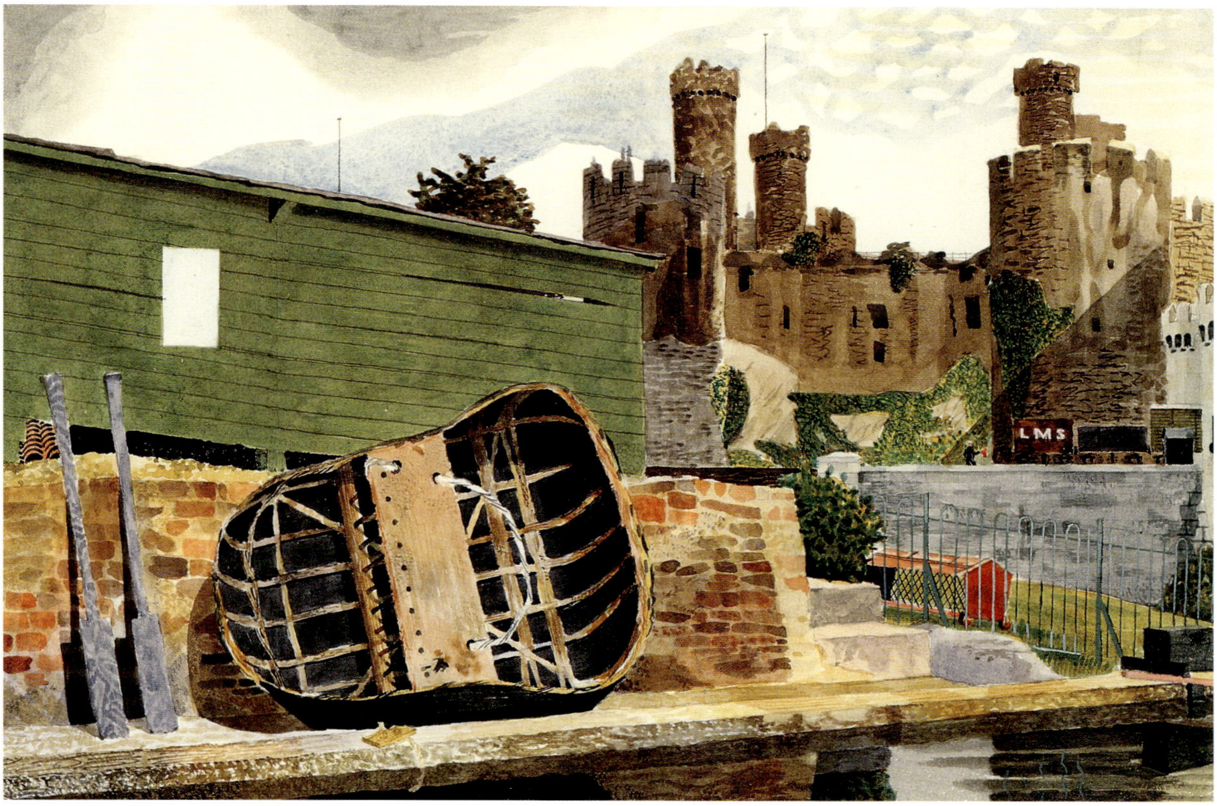

17 Conway Castle and Coracle, Caernarvonshire *c.*1940
Watercolour on paper
31.5 x 49 cms (12.5 x 19.25 inches)
Board of Trustees of the Victoria and Albert Museum,
London (E.2419-1949)

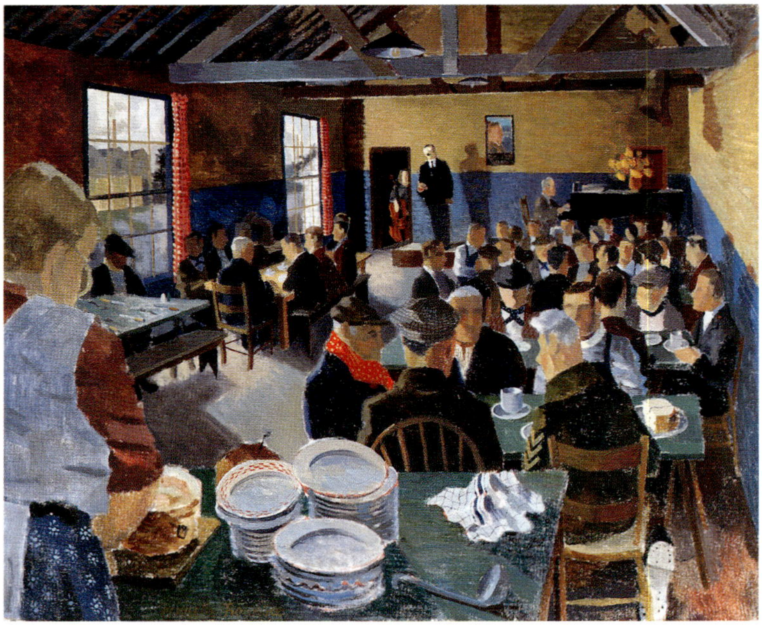

18 CEMA Canteen Concert, Isle of Dogs, London E14 1941
Oil on canvas
60.9 x 76.2 cms (27.25 x 30 inches)
The Imperial War Museum, London
(IMW:ART LD 1879)

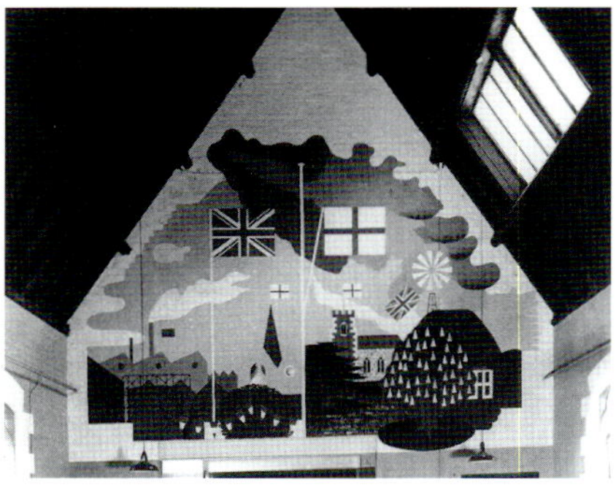

19 The British Restaurant at Acton *c.*1943
Photograph
The Witt Library,
The Courtauld Institute of Art, London

Equally evocative of wartime is *The Railway Carriage, Blackout* (Fig.20), painted in about 1942, progressing with anxious passengers and lights out beneath a railway arch.

The effort to record Britain was at its height by 1942.[29] Recording Britain had amassed 727 watercolours when it held an exhibition at the National Gallery in June 1944, including work by Sutherland, Piper, Keith Vaughan, Leonard Rosoman and Henry Moore.

When Rowntree responded to the opportunity to provide a mural for a wartime *British Restaurant at Acton* in 1943 (Fig.19), he took a significant step towards design and away from recording what he saw. Whilst the *CEMA Concert* painting recorded British wartime life, it made no attempt to organise or change it. The mural at Acton was different in purpose and style – a more overtly persuasive art designed to celebrate and promote loyalty to British values and cultural identity, assertive and stylised like a poster, its clean colour and sharp lines brightening up a dull interior whilst promoting a crisp image of rural England, at right, and of urban factories, at left. These are the great stock themes of propaganda: industry and agriculture, modern times and historic identity, town and country working together for the wealth and security of all. This was Rowntree's closest approach to official art, and it retains all the pleasant freshness of a good, promotional travel poster with not a tank or battle in sight. Only the barrage balloon denotes a time of conflict.

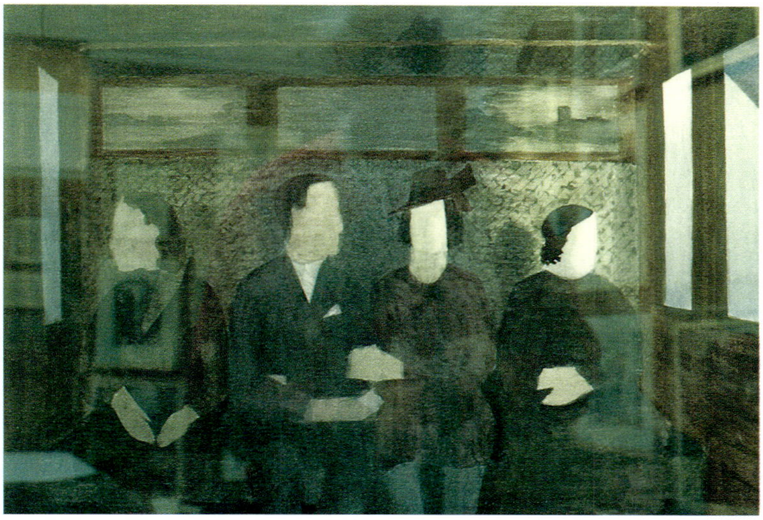

20 The Railway Carriage, Blackout *c.*1942
Watercolour on paper
30.2 x 42.7 cms (11.75 x 16.5 inches)
The Fry Public Art Gallery,
Saffron Walden, Essex

Stylistically this was a new development and the first evidence of much that was to follow. Since Rowntree was constructing an image from predetermined elements, each a visual sign in itself, for example images of industry, faith and nationality (factory, church and flags), rather than observing the fall of light on objects before him, his images could be as flat as road signs with all forms parallel to the wall surface. The effect is heraldic: fully modelled realism would have been less effective. Rowntree's sense of rhythm and pattern came to the fore. As the overall shape of the sky in this mural derived from deliberate brushmarks, the design was probably enlarged from a study on paper or card. This new visual language which has suddenly sprung into existence appears simplified and diagrammatic. It includes many stylistic references, not least to contemporary French mural painting and tapestries, which in turn developed devices from both Cubism and the Middle Ages, yet the curling cloud recalls Paul Nash and Edward Burra's response to Surrealism.

Rowntree was also addressing a different audience, providing colour in a mundane setting for people who would not necessarily recognise its cultural reference points. This called for maximum legibility from a distance, simplification and an instantly recognisable catalogue of images. Only the early *Homage to French Culture in the Nineteenth Century* had attempted such a catalogue effect, addressing its message to a mass of viewers and to the Ministry of Information who paid for it.

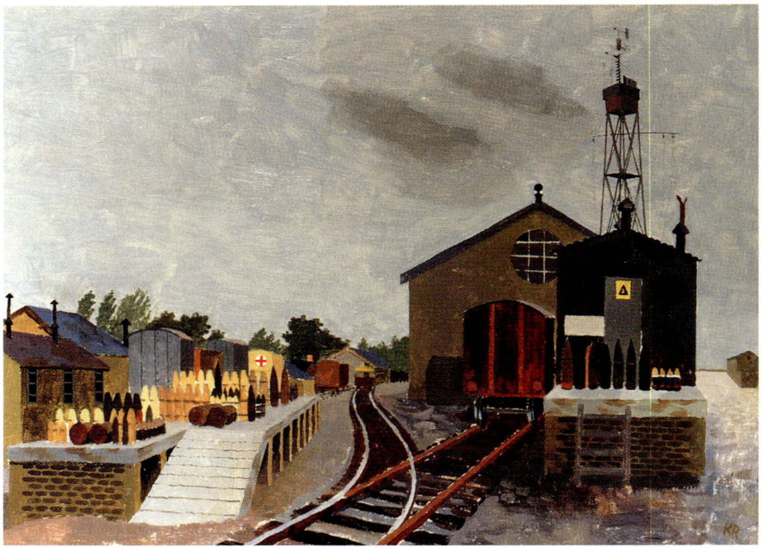

21 Experimental Establishment, Shoeburyness *c.*1945
(also known as *The Government Ordnance Establishment*)
Oil on canvas; Signed *KR*
31.8 x 53.3 cms (12.5 x 21 inches)
The Imperial War Museum, London
(IMW:ART LD 5690)

The opportunity changed Rowntree's painting. It led to new commissions for murals and these established in him a stylised and geometric visual language.[30] It provided an alternative source of income, and a third way of working alongside the watercolours for Recording Britain and canvases for the WAAC. The whole idea of signs and signboards fascinated him: he loved the lettering in churches and the signwriter's art. Kenneth Clark was well aware of this. On 14 November 1944 he wrote to Rowntree with a private commission: 'Would you like to do a commission for me? It is a view of Holly Hill, Hampstead, including the Benskins pub sign. I could show you the subject which appeals to me if you come to lunch one day. I am much afraid that the Town Council will widen this road and may remove the Benskins sign, which is one of the best of its kind. But after your series at Barclays, perhaps you are getting sick of brewers signs.'[31] He had made a watercolour of *The Signwriter's Shop, Southwark*, with plentiful evidence of work, for Barclay's brewery in homage to the skills and beauty of a downmarket branch of painting that he greatly respected.[32]

In the same letter Kenneth Clark also discussed John Piper, whom Rowntree admired. A small painting by Piper, *Micheldever Station*, shows a comparable love of railways, signs and architectural façades, though Piper painted it more loosely with the dramatic stormy effect of the New Romantic painters. Rowntree saw the study reproduced in the *Architectural Review* and was so taken with it that he wrote to Piper asking if he could buy it. Piper sent Rowntree the original and refused payment. Piper's involvement in war art is evident in Clark's letter: 'He is doing magnificent work for the War Artists at present and I do not

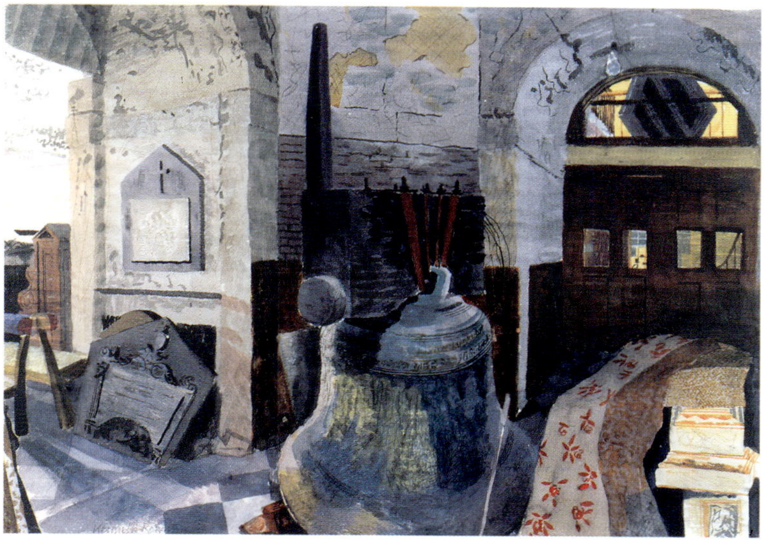

22 St James' Church, Piccadilly, London, W1 1944
Watercolour on paper
Signed *Kenneth Rowntree*
55.8 x 38.7 cms (22 x 15.25 inches)
The Imperial War Museum, London
(IMW:ART LD 5022)

know how much time he could give to non-war subjects, but we might try and get first refusal of anything he does on his next leave.'[33]

Rowntree also painted war subjects. For example, *The Experimental Establishment, Shoeburyness, 1945: Firing Through Screens*, is a mass of machinery, cranes, guns, railway tracks, sheds and six tall pylons of the experimental radio unit. Its companion piece, *The Experimental Establishment, Shoeburyness* (Fig.21), which shows railway sidings neatly stacked with shells and explosives prepared for loading onto trains, is a mundane scene with the wind blustering among the trees beneath a grey sky. Sheds and explosives cover the platform.

There are two watercolours in the Imperial War Museum that are linked to his work for the WAAC and Recording Britain. Both are wartime interiors of *St James' Church, Piccadilly, London W1* (Fig.22), the church which stands opposite the Royal Academy of Art and is often called the artists' church. In 1944 Rowntree made a view along the nave seen through a doorway in which calm, cleanliness and light predominate, but the second watercolour, made two years later, is the disturbing assemblage of a bomb-damaged interior. The church which Rowntree had enjoyed as a haven of calm, is suddenly a confused tangle of damaged objects scarcely recognisable in their shadowy new relationships. Paul Nash and Henry Moore had both adapted this technique to depict the dislocation of war. Graham Sutherland and John Piper made it into a romantic human drama expressed in ruined buildings, dark skies and encroaching growth. Rowntree is closer to Nash, or the poetic wartime works of Eric Ravilious, to whom he paid homage in an etching of 1944.

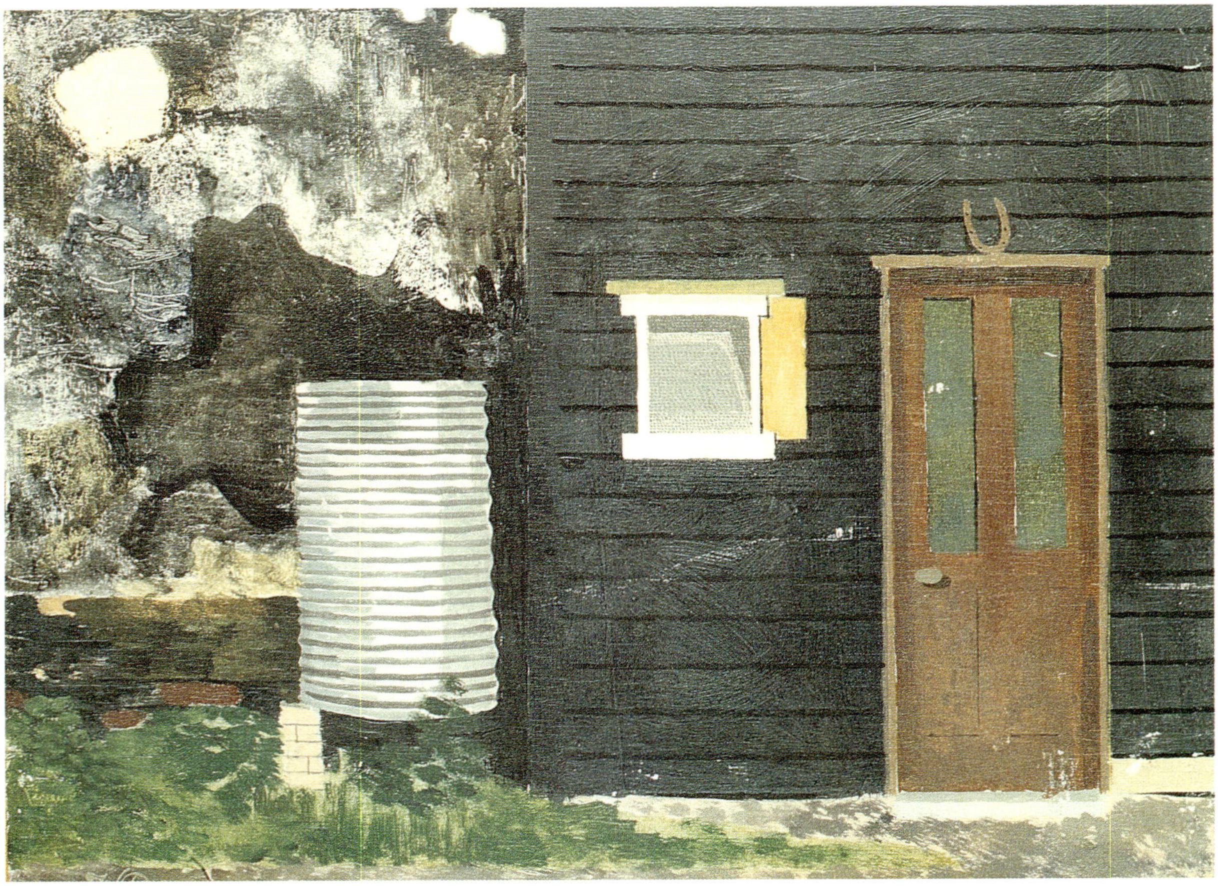

23 Back door, larder window and water-butt 1945
(also known as *Water-Butt, 'Simpkins'*)
Oil on canvas
33 x 44 cms (13 x 17.25 inches)
The Fry Public Art Gallery,
Saffron Walden, Essex

End of War

In the last years of the war, Rowntree looked forward to the future, working for an exhibition at the Leicester Galleries in 1946. The catalogue listed twenty-five paintings from 1945, their subjects on the whole intimate, domestic and personal – a relief from the official demands of WAAC commissions, Recording Britain, or public murals. Not one of the titles listed for 1945 refers to warfare, with the possible exception of *Desolate Hotel* (cat.no.49), and many of them celebrated private life in Essex, including *Essex Farm* and *Back door, larder window and water-butt* (Fig.23).

In 1942 a son, Adam, had been born to Kenneth and Diana, demanding a further change in their accommodation. They had moved from Great Bardfield to a pink farmhouse, 'Simpkins', at Lindsell in the next village.[34] *Back door, larder window and water-butt* was painted at this house. Parallel, as usual, to the picture plane, the door, window and water-butt are presented as a sequence of forms in which incidental effects humanise the whole. The water-butt is propped up on bricks. The larder window has a yellow rectangle at right but its ventilation window is open inwards behind a perforated screen minutely depicted with tiny dots to achieve the effect of transparency. The brown door has a horseshoe above it for luck. Rowntree has painted each nail hole in the horseshoe and just enough shadow to its left to make it lean safely against the wooden black-painted wall. Another painting at Lindsell from 1945 was the dark interior view with a nude recorded in *Lamplight* (Fig.24).

The end of the war in 1945 freed Rowntree from both the restraints and opportunities that wartime commissions entailed. He now had to use the contacts and discoveries that he had made to fashion an independent career. His exhibition at the Leicester Galleries, Leicester Square in 1946 shows how rapid Rowntree's adjustment was. He was, after all, a family man and his output was suddenly both necessary and prolific.[35]

Exhibitions

The Leicester Galleries prepared a contract, which Rowntree signed on 15 August 1946, to present an exhibition in the 'large rooms' of the gallery in November of the same year. Rowntree showed a total of

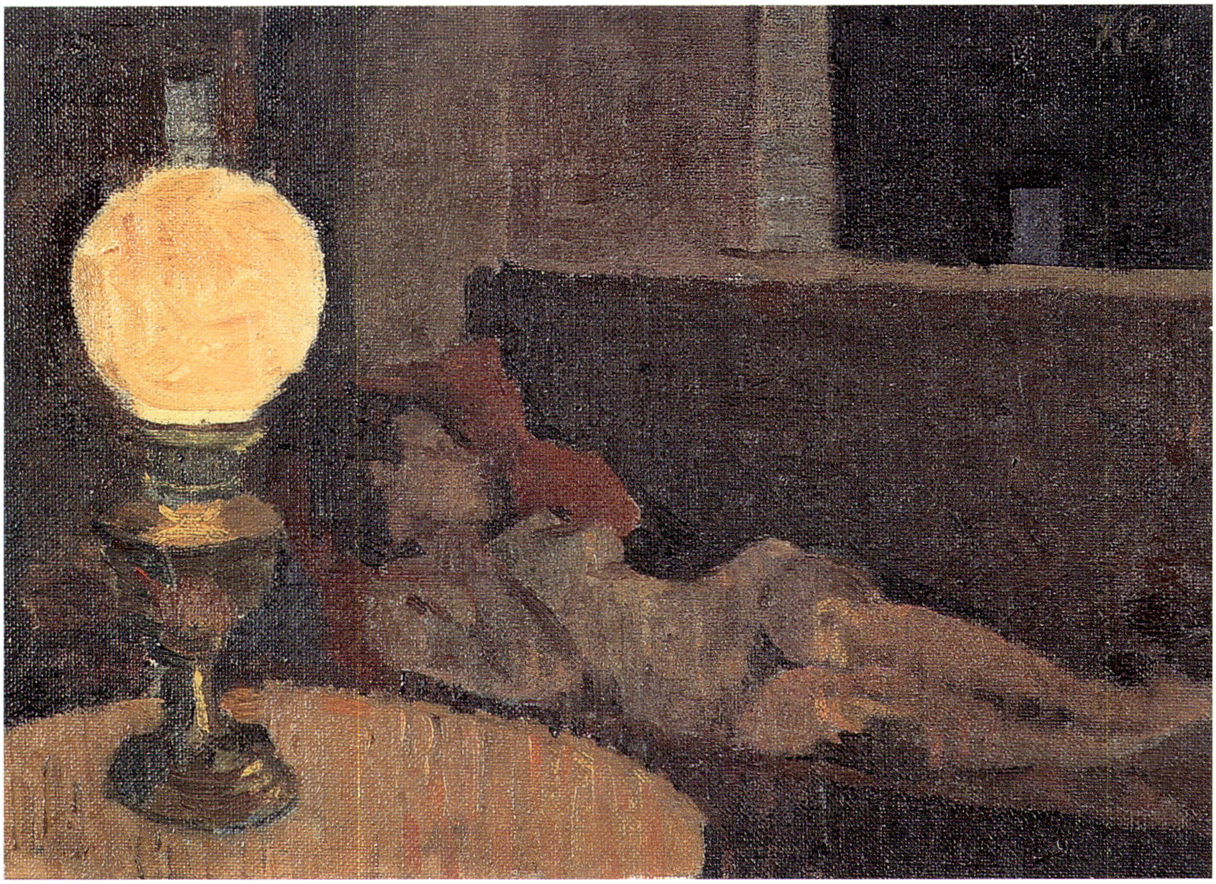

24 Lamplight 1945
Oil on board
28 x 38.1cms (11 x 15 inches)

sixty-one works dating from 1938 to 1946. He was now thirty-one and the exhibition was in itself a valuable sign of recognition. Seventeen works dated from 1946, including a *Cornish Landscape*[36] which is probably the painting now in the Tate Gallery.[37]

Before the Leicester Galleries' one-man show opened, Rowntree had contributed to a mixed exhibition at the City of Leicester Art Gallery, 16 February–31 March 1946, under the title *1946 Spring Contemporaries*. It provided a context within which to assess his work. As Trevor Thomas explained in the catalogue introduction, 'for the period of hostilities artists in this country were virtually cut off from dominant continental influences.' He went on to wonder 'if there were any comparable signs, as apparently among composers, of a renaissance of active traditions.'[38] All of this was evident in Rowntree's development since 1939. Thomas discerned, too, what Rowntree's Acton mural and *Cornish Landscape* shared: 'a desire to return to the primitive. The term primitive was not equivalent to crude, rude or undeveloped but regarded as primary and elemental, simpler and unaffected, and involving almost a longing for an original innocence before taste and feeling were vitiated and polluted by industrialised living.'[39]

Rowntree exhibited among twenty-six artists, including Edward Burra, Robert Colquhoun, Ivon Hitchens, L. S. Lowry, Henry Moore, Rodrigo Moynihan, Paul Nash, Ben Nicholson, Victor Pasmore, John Piper, Michael Rothenstein, Julian Trevelyan and John Tunnard. The prices reveal each artist's confidence or fame. Rowntree's prices ranged from twenty guineas (£21) to thirty guineas (£31 10s) but the highest price by far was Victor Pasmore's oil painting *Moonrise* of 1945, for sale at 300 guineas (£315), ten times the price of a Rowntree. Ben Nicholson charged only £38 for *674-1945*, a work in oil and pencil. That must have encouraged Rowntree. To her amazement, about 1946–7, Kenneth bought Diana Rowntree two Nicholsons including *Carbis Bay 5919* of 1945 and a small *Abstract* that showed Nicholson's response to geometric painting and in particular to the works of Mondrian whom he had known in Hampstead during the war.

Although there was much here that was extraordinary and new, not least in the paintings by Nicholson and Pasmore, Rowntree realised that he could thrive in this context. On the other hand, his one-man show at the Leicester Galleries in London could launch him on the London art world. The gallery charged one third commission, which was not unusual in London. Kenneth Rowntree's first one-man show was underway within a year of the war ending. It was a quick adjustment to new opportunities in which commercial galleries and private buyers replaced government projects.

III Post-War

In 1947 Kenneth Rowntree designed book covers and much of his book design was essentially escapist. The Pilot Press provided the opportunity. This small publishing venture was the creation of John Howard, the husband of the journalist and writer Marghanita Laski. Rowntree entered fully into the narrator's role when designing these covers, providing an atmospheric glimpse of the story inside the book. He made good use of the front, spine and back to establish the continuity of his narrative, though this is deceptive when the dust jacket is displayed flat as the initial image is at the right and not, as it might be in a painting, to the left.

His dust jacket for Louis Aragon's *Passengers of Destiny* (Fig.26) is a lively evening scene in a French town. Figures stroll by in the foreground with umbrellas. The design is a distant echo of the Impressionist painter Caillebotte's *Place de l'Europe on a Rainy Day*, but Rowntree adapts the scene radically to his own ends. Behind the strolling figures the omnibus silhouettes the passengers inside – one on top seen against the sky between the shadowy forms of buildings. The bus is halted by a traffic policeman at the intersection. A French flag flies from the building behind him. These two motifs fall exactly on the spine of the book, to be visible on the shelf as succinct identifiers of the novel. At left (the back cover) a bus departs with sinister figures seen against the last of the daylight, as urban and anonymous as any by the Surrealist René Magritte.

A different approach was adopted for a cover Rowntree designed for *The Listener* magazine in November 1947. The romance of communication travels from the microphone and transmitter to shipping at sea in the daylight and to the house ablaze with light in the dark night. Textured shapes project the lettering. This design is closer to the approach of Ravilious, the friend whose plane had vanished on a wartime air-sea rescue mission in 1942.[40] It contrasts with the Aragon

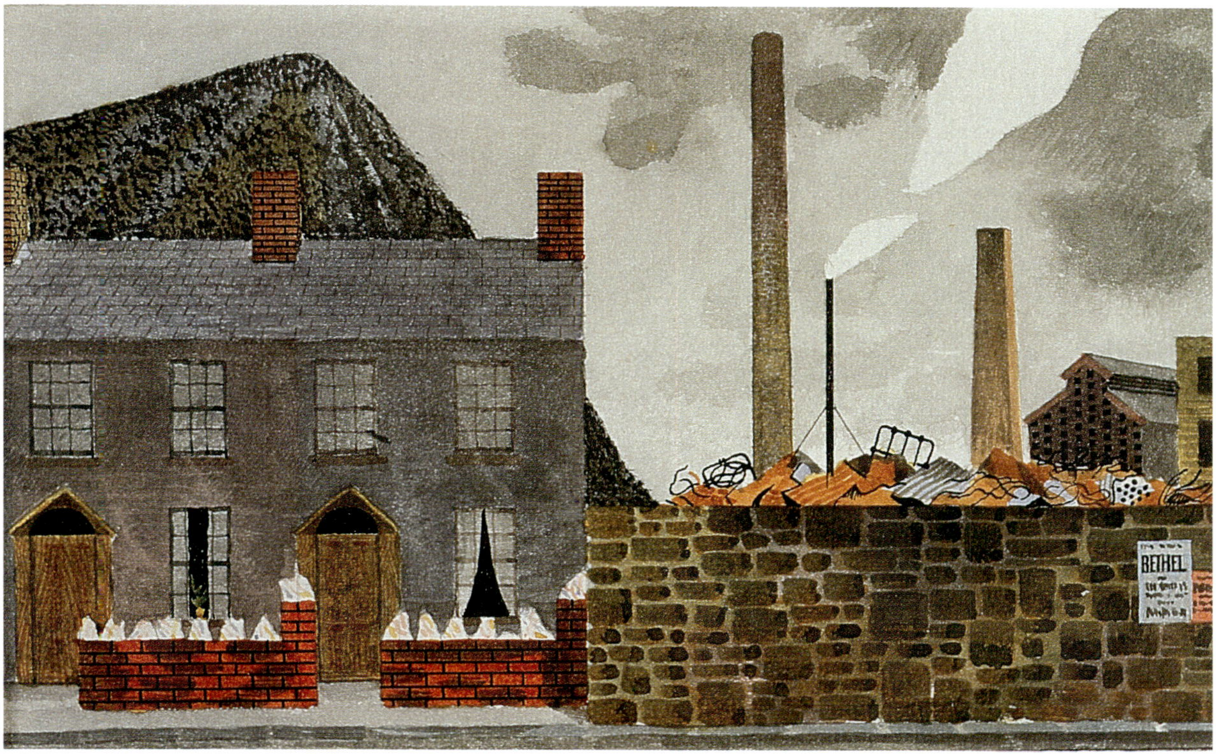

25 South Wales Landscape, Glamorgan 1948
Watercolour on paper
For *A Prospect of Wales* 1948
15.2 x 24cms (6 x 9.5 inches)
The National Library of Wales, Aberystwyth

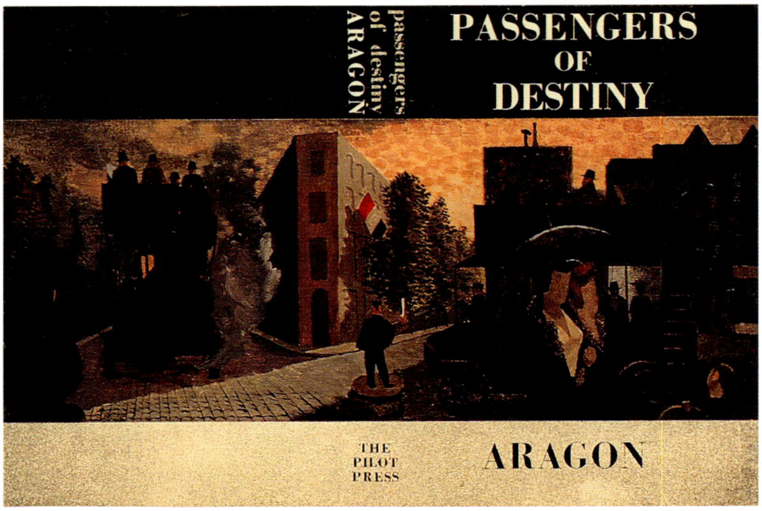

26 Passengers of Destiny,
Louis Aragon 1947
(Aragon's *Les voyageurs de l'Impériale*,
translated by Hannah Josephson)
Book cover for Pilot Press, London
22.5 x 34.5 cms (9 x 13.5 inches)

cover which was a painted narrative. This second approach was used again for an unpublished Pilot Press project done in about 1948. It retold the story of *Maria Marten, or the Murder in the Red Barn* in sequential scenes from right to left, a kind of joined up illustration, acting as a titillating sample. Rowntree's cover for *Wennon* (Fig.27) by Cledwyn Hughes was published in 1948 without the clever use of the spine seen earlier. Nevertheless Rowntree's scenes could not have been more dramatic, with the speeding van leaping from the road and crashing through the crossing gates split seconds before the train passes. Finally Leo Walmsley's *Master Mariner* (Fig.28) came out with Collins in London in a dust jacket that combined narrative with elegant graphics. Again there are sections, top and bottom dominated by inventive lettering. In between is the imagery of the ship's deck, as stylised, geometric and parallel to the surface as any of the motifs in the Acton mural. There are hints of Le Corbusier, the Swiss architect who so admired the architecture of ships, and forms that might come from the French cubist Léger or from an English Surrealist like Wadsworth, but the whole effect moves with the action as the ship steams past the white cliffs, the little houses by the shore and the green fields above the chalk face.

On one last cover Rowntree was most explicit in his cubist borrowings and at the same time most personal about his own concerns. This was the King Penguin book *A Prospect of Wales* (Fig.29) in which watercolours of Wales accompanied a text by Gwyn Jones. Uniquely the book acknowledges the painter before the writer [41] and Rowntree made for it a spectacular cover signed 'KR'. In rich colouring, this cover depicts Wales sunlit on the front and raining on the back cover. It is a complex construction in layers.

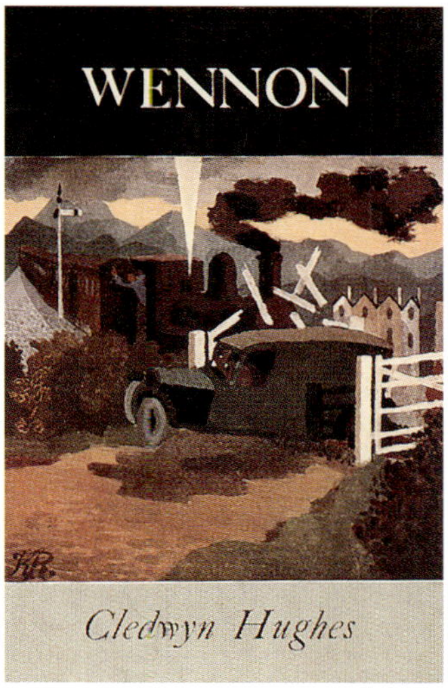

27 **Wennon**, Cledwyn Hughes 1948
Book cover for Pilot Press, London
19.5 x 13 cms (8.75 x 5.25 inches)

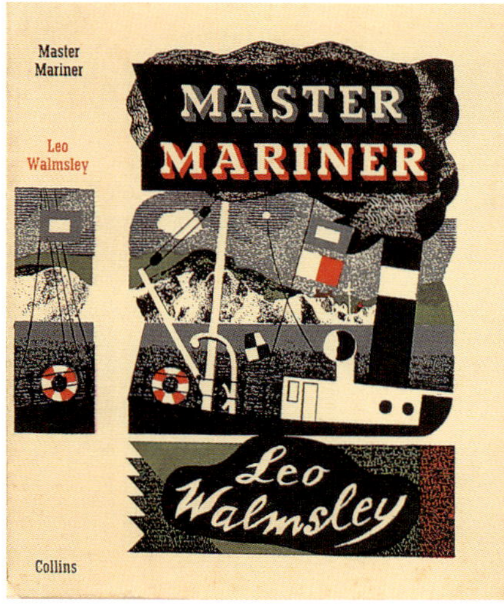

28 **Master Mariner**, Leo Walmsley 1948
Book cover for Collins, London
20.5 x 17.5 cms (9.75 x 7 inches)

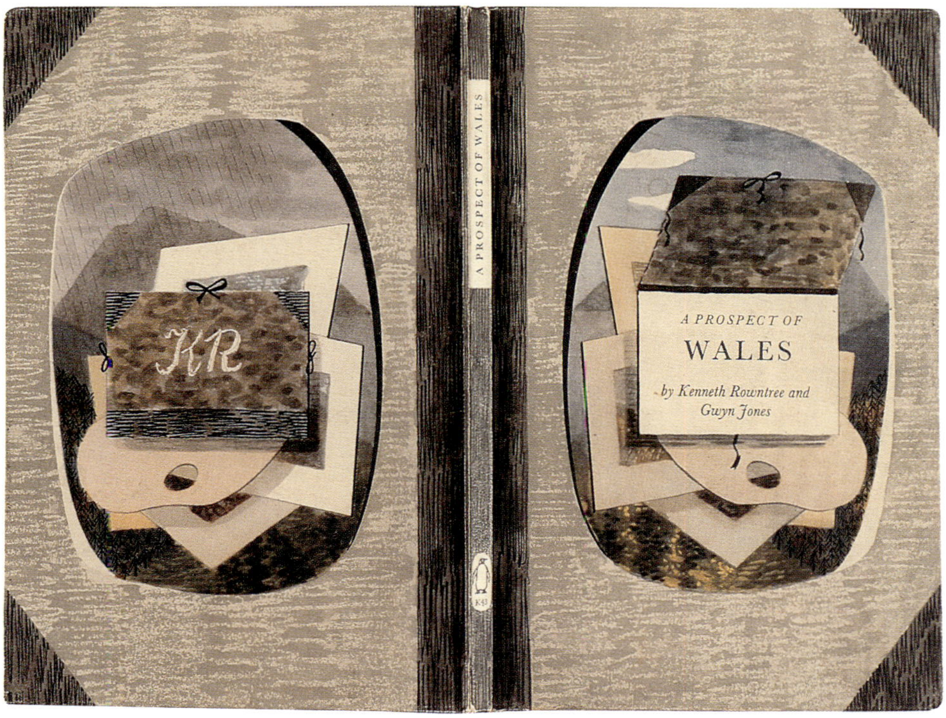

29 **A Prospect of Wales** 1948
Book cover for Penguin Press (King Penguin), London
18.5 x 25 cms (7.25 x 9.75 inches)

The little book is designed to look like a portfolio with strengthened corners and textured surface originally made in watercolour over waxed lines. On these surfaces Rowntree has set two disk shapes bearing the main imagery. On the front cover, clouds hang in a clear sky above the mountain. Four watercolours and a palette are overlapped and, in front of all of them, a portfolio opens to reveal the title and authors of the book. The whole activity of painting on the hills and coasts of Wales is connected with the idea of the book as a portfolio opening up for the reader. On the back cover, he has closed the portfolio, as the book is closed, and pencilled rain falls from the grey skies onto the hillside.

Inside the book the designer gives way to the painter with reproductions of watercolours of Wales. In technique they belong to Recording Britain and range from the grandest romantic ruins, including *The Bishop's Palace, St. David's* (Pembrokeshire), to *Caernarvon Castle* and *Hafod (Cardiganshire)*, but in others the drama of landscape dominates, as in *The Snowdon Range* or *Mynydd Mawr Range*. Nondescript houses appear across the *Estuary near Portmadoc (Caernarvonshire)* or *Looking up the Traeth Mawr*. The balance of buildings and landscape shifts image by image: in *Autumn Landscape, Merionethshire* the folded valley and granite farmhouse recall Gauguin's Brittany. In others it is the houses that assert identity, in *St David's looking towards Ramsey Island (Pembrokeshire)*, in *Parc Cright in Clouds (Merionethshire)* or in individual portraits of buildings, from *Mrs. Siddon's Birthplace, Brecon* to three chapels and a hillside in *School at Upper Corris*. In the bleakest street scene, *South Wales Landscape, Glamorgan* (Fig.25) grimly uniform, grey terrace houses back onto a vast, precarious and lifeless slag heap where chimneys stand guard over scrap heaps of rusting metal. By contrast, the welcoming *View from the Hotel of the Gyffarllwyd Falls, Devil's Bridge (Cardiganshire)* (Fig.30) is an elevated view of mountains and forests in the clean air. The twenty-one originals were exhibited as *A Prospect of Wales* by the Arts Council in Cardiff in 1949, the year after publication. Gwyn Jones in his catalogue introduction noted that, 'Kenneth Rowntree has, for the most part, avoided the oft-sung show pieces of Wales.' Jones said the watercolours reveal, 'the familiar seen through new eyes, the everyday made significant by vision and craftsmanship.'[42]

The book included several drawings of clasped hands on a rain-lashed tombstone, of sheep in a field overshadowed by a slag heap with a discarded metal bedhead in a broken stone wall, and a coal truck inscribed *Tredegar*, behind are lines of miners' dwellings that resemble

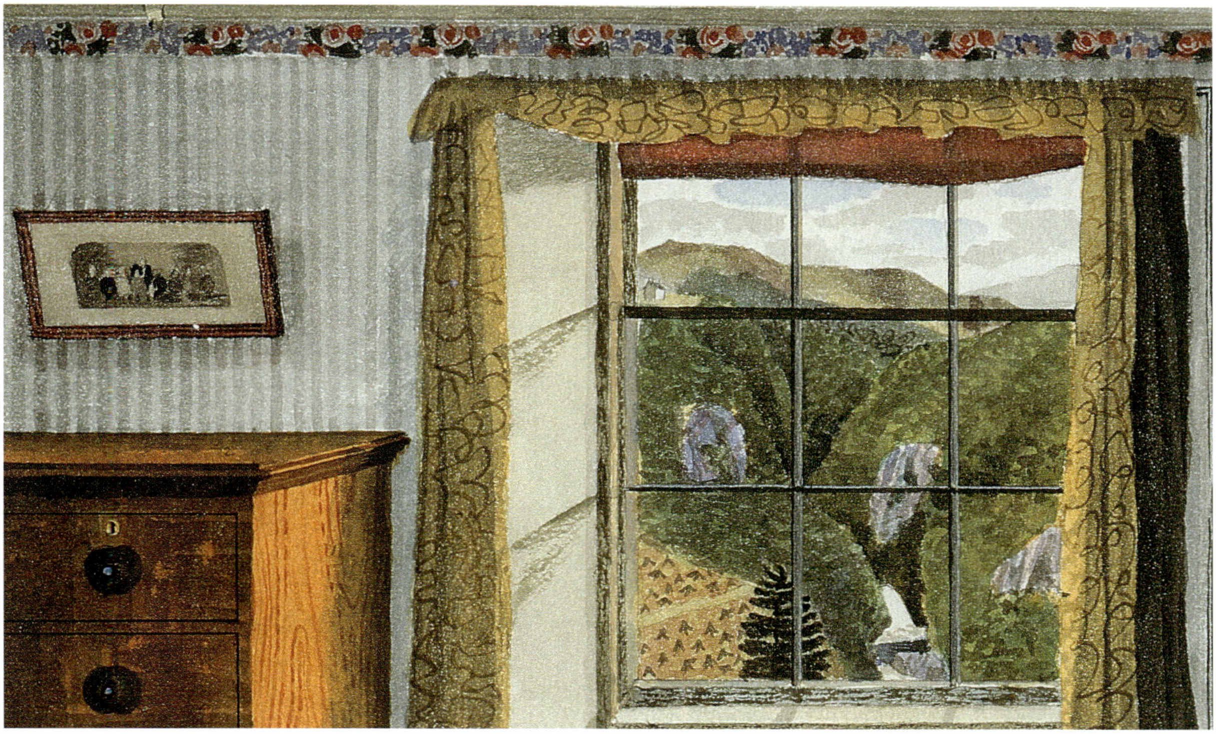

30 View from the Hotel of the Gyffarllwyd Falls, Devil's Bridge (Cardiganshire) 1948
Watercolour on paper. For *A Prospect of Wales* 1948
15 x 24.2 cms (6 x 9.75 inches)
The National Library of Wales, Aberystwyth

trains crossing the hillside. During 1948, a *Memorial Exhibition of the work of Eric Ravilious* was held at Eastbourne and Brighton. The loss of Ravilious in the war meant for Rowntree the loss of a mentor and friend whose work he admired. His vignette wood engravings with which the memorial catalogue cover was decorated may be directly compared with Rowntree's Welsh drawings although Rowntree's vision is more frank and less romantic.[43]

Murals, exhibitions and books were all used by Rowntree to make his art public in the early post-war years. In none of them was he working wholly for himself. His next opportunity was in many ways decisive for his development. He had completed several murals and joined the Society of Mural Painters. In 1949 Robin Darwin, the Rector of the Royal College of Art, invited Rowntree to head its mural painting studios. The Rowntrees returned to London with Kenneth in one of the most significant establishments for the teaching of art. But the Royal College of Art, then housed in buildings adjacent to the Victoria and Albert Museum, was distinguished by another feature from all the other

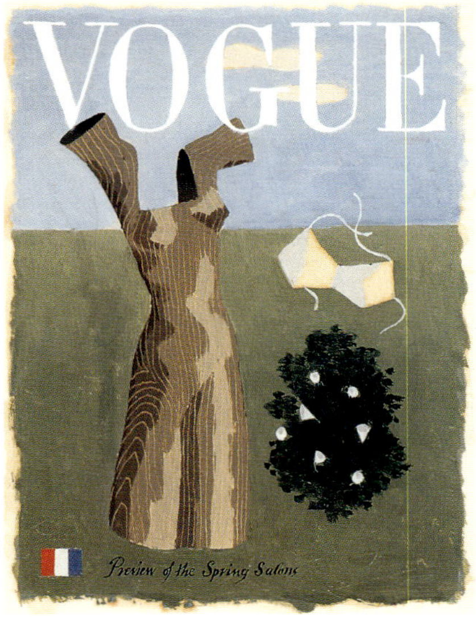

31 Preview of the Spring Salons *c.*1958
Projected design for *Vogue*
Oil on card
31.7 x 24.1 cms (12.5 x 9.5 inches)

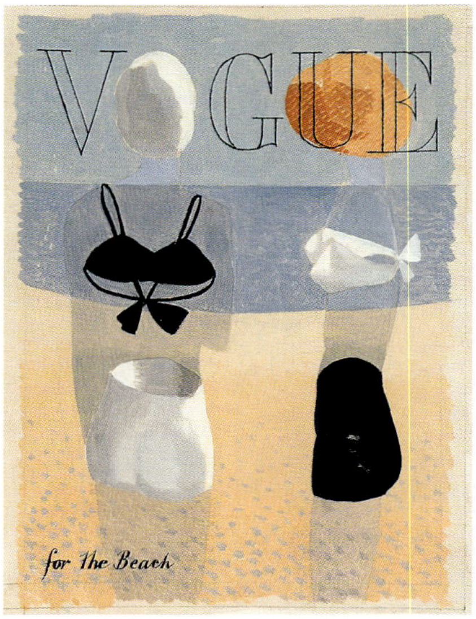

32 For the Beach *c.*1958
Projected design for *Vogue*
Oil on card
31.7 x 24.1 cms (12.5 x 9.5 inches)

London colleges of art. The Royal College of Art, then as now, was primarily a design institute, a context which for Rowntree meant that his painting must adapt to aspects of design. The mural at Acton had already demanded changes in approach and some of his book covers were clearly works of graphic design. The painterly approach of the *Leicester Galleries' exhibition* of 1946 confronted the demand to reconcile art and design. Kenneth, Diana and the young Adam moved to Putney, to a house by the Thames with a spacious studio designed by Diana from four attic rooms.

Tendencies visible right across post-war Europe promoted an architectonic, geometric approach to painting. Already in the 1930s Nicholson had contributed to the publication *Circle* alongside architects and constructivists. War had brought geometric artists to London, including, if only briefly, Mondrian. Not far away, at Lawn Road Flats, Jack Pritchard was encouraging Bauhaus contacts as Gropius, Moholy-Nagy and others passed through. By 1949 non-representational art was no longer new in London. Victor Pasmore, for example, at Camberwell School of Art, published an anthology called *Abstract Art: Comments by some Artists and Critics*, with statements from Kenneth and Mary Martin, Terry Frost, Anthony Hill and others.[44]

Whilst Rowntree did not rush to develop his art in this way – after all his figurative paintings and landscapes were now making his name – he had, in 1946, exhibited alongside Pasmore and Nicholson.[45] Since the 1930s the reconciliation of art and design had become increasingly visible. Diana Rowntree was acutely aware of this and Kenneth was nevertheless mixing with designers and architects as well as painters at a metropolitan centre for creative research. He often met old friends Robert Goodden and Hugh Casson, both architects, in the College's Senior Common Room in the Cromwell Road.

In 1949 the architects, Yorke, Rosenberg and Mardall, commissioned a mural for the Barclay School in Stevenage. This didactic mural survives, displaying the geometric forms of the right-angled triangle (2:3:4) for the Theorem of Pythagoras and a translucent cone demonstrating its geometric sections. Triangular trees, not seen since the Acton mural, flourish and in the distance stands a barn that frequently reappears in later works, comprising a side view and elevation flattened into a single image. A catalogue published in 1950 describes the mural as completed.[46] It was the most geometric landscape yet produced by Rowntree, who was encouraged here perhaps by working with architects designing for school pupils.

Rowntree's synthesis of painting and design offered the viewer the satisfaction of translating his images, rather like solving a puzzle. The most enjoyable of these were projected covers for *Vogue* magazine made in 1950. These are provocative puzzles at once severe, Surrealist, and warmly enjoyable. *Preview of the Spring Salons* (Fig.31) has Rowntree's most adventurous images yet of animated but empty clothes. Their lightness against the blue sky and grass suggest the lively woman who might wear them. In each case the letter *O* of *Vogue* is a head. The second Spring figure (with bikini top) turns into a bush. *For the Beach* (Fig.32) presents silvery shadows of women who almost materialise. The *O* is both a head and a strange cloud (a double visual pun). We can see inside these empty clothes, through the back view and side view, but their light and colour maintain a carefree summer mood. With *Autumn Tweeds* (Fig.33) the Constructive approach gives way to painterly effects, whilst *Christmas Parties* (Fig.34) may be autobiographical as Sasha (see Fig.35), the Rowntrees' daughter, was born in 1947, about the right age for this image by this date. These unused projects mark out positions between an intellectual Constructive approach and a painterly approach. Rowntree wavered in his search for a synthesis.

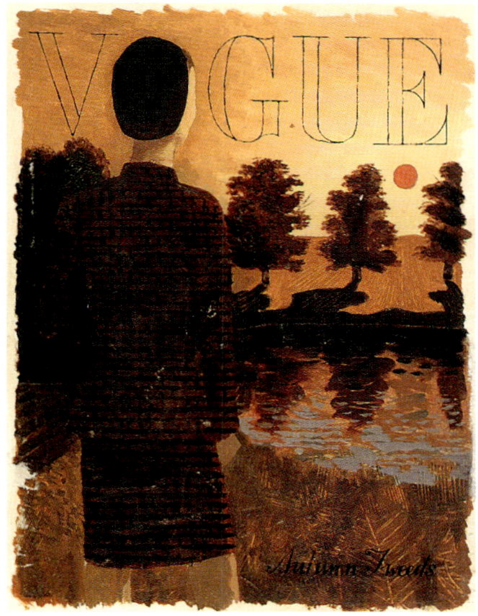

33 Autumn Tweeds *c.*1958
Projected design for *Vogue*
Oil on card
31.7 x 24.1 cms (12.5 x 9.5 inches)

He exhibited twice in November 1950, firstly at an *Exhibition of Paintings by the Visitors and Staff of the Ruskin School of Drawing and Fine Art*, 7–18 November, with slightly increased prices, offering *Spring, Essex* for thirty-five guineas and *Cornish Landscape* for forty-five guineas. The other exhibitors included Albert Rutherston (145 guineas) and Barnett Freedman (150 guineas). The Ashmolean Museum lent works by Pasmore, and there were also paintings by Claude Rogers, Rodrigo Moynihan and John Minton.

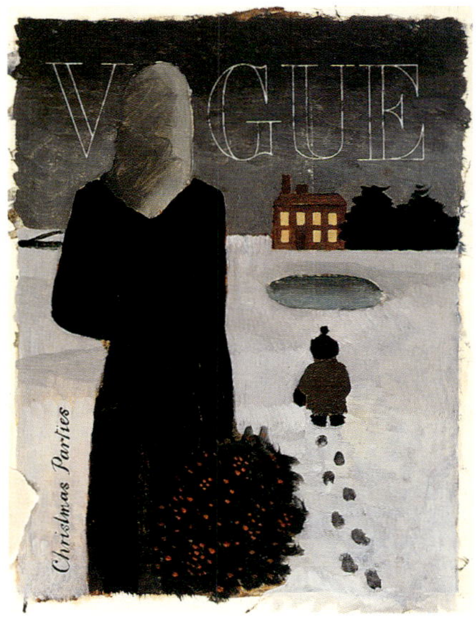

34 Christmas Parties *c.*1958
Projected design for *Vogue*
Oil on card
31.7 x 24.1 cms (12.5 x 9.5 inches)

Secondly, at the Leicester Galleries in November 1950, he showed watercolours in the Entrance Gallery. The thirty-six works included *Evening Bather*, *Bather at Aberystwyth* and *Storm over the Cathedral, Canterbury* (Fig.36), characteristic post-war paintings reflecting little of his new London life, emphasising instead rural scenes in Essex, Suffolk and Kent.

Four artists who showed at the *Ruskin School* exhibition were teaching at the Royal College in 1951. They figure in the large canvas by Rodrigo Moynihan *Portrait Group (The Teaching Staff of the Painting School at the Royal College of Art, 1949–50)*, finished in 1951 (Fig.37). At the left sits John Minton, whom Rowntree also depicted in a brilliant study at this time seated in a theatre box surrounded by much the same

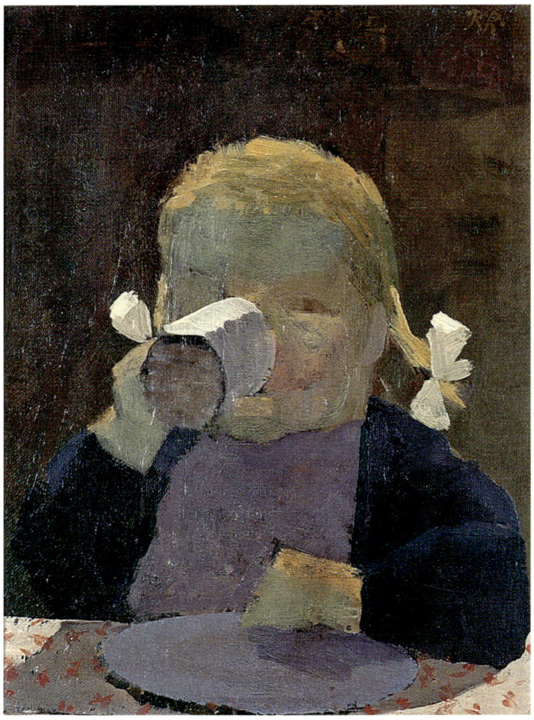

35 Portrait of Sasha aged four 1951
Oil on canvas
35.5 x 27.9 cms (14 x 11 inches)

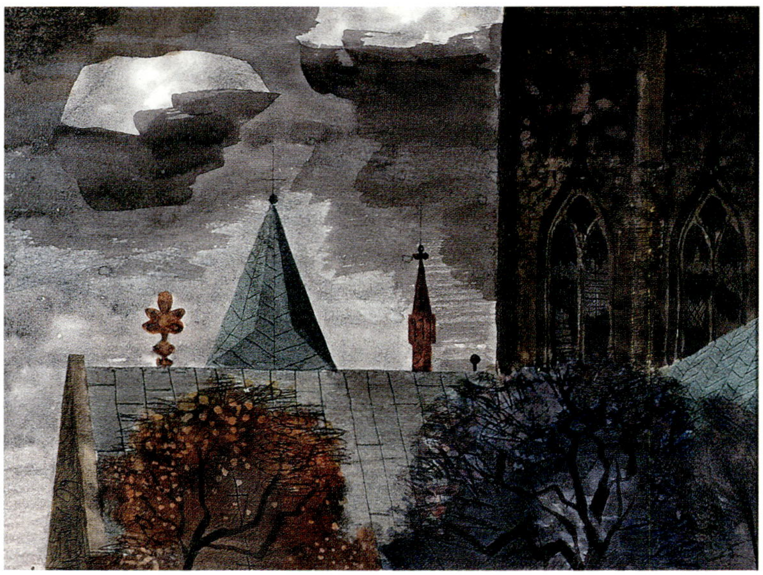

36 Storm over the Cathedral, Canterbury 1950
Watercolour and inks on paper
22.9 x 30.5 cms (9 x 12 inches)
Collection John and Lesley Milner

isolation (Fig.38). Then come four standing figures: Colin Hayes, Carel Weight, Rodney Burn and Robert Buhler. Finally there are four seated figures: Charles Mahoney, Kenneth Rowntree, Ruskin Spear (on the couch) and Moynihan himself. Here is Rowntree in the setting where he worked for ten years. Minton was experimental but a New Romantic. He has his place, and if he looks intent and serious, so do all the others in this inscrutable *Portrait Group*.

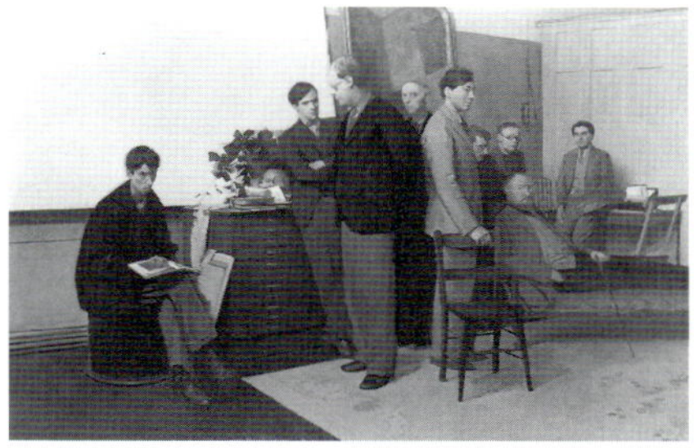

37 Rodrigo Moynihan
Portrait Group
(The Teaching Staff of the Painting School at the Royal College of Art, 1949-50) 1951
Oil on canvas
213.3 x 334.1 cms (84 x 132 inches)
The Tate Gallery, London

The year 1951 presented great opportunities for the Royal College of Art and for Rowntree. Hugh Casson, Professor of Interior Design at the College, played a central role in the Festival of Britain staged on the south bank of the Thames opposite Charing Cross Station, to celebrate surviving World War II and to launch Britain into an optimistic era of reconstruction. Hugh Casson knew that the *Lion and Unicorn Pavilion* in particular could be a showpiece for the Royal College of Art and he deliberately gave projects to College staff. Within sight of the Dome of Discovery and its Skylon, the *Lion and Unicorn Pavilion* occupied a busy site. The architects of the pavilion were Professors Richard D. Russell and Robert Goodden who designed doves of peace suspended from the roof of the hall that celebrated British freedoms. Here was a large mural by Edward Bawden opposite a long *Freedom* mural (Fig.39) by Rowntree, illustrating *Freedom of Worship*, *Democratic Freedom* and *Freedom under the Law*. His most important public commission to date was seen by many thousands of visitors.

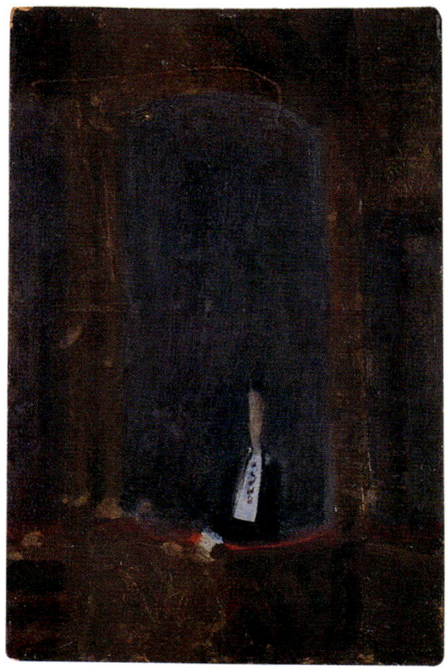

38 John Minton in a Box
at Her Majesty's Theatre 1950–1
Oil on board
30.5 x 20.4 cms (12 x 8 inches)

A small study for the *Freedom* mural survives, prepared for transcription onto the curved surface erected in front of the wall of the pavilion. Laurie Lee wrote a commentary in which the propaganda purpose of the festival is clearly detectable: 'The British people are something more than the sum of men with ancestors, children in schools, families in homes and gardens, and patients in hospitals. They are, in addition, compositions of various particular habits, attitudes, instincts, qualities and characteristic moods.'[47] He roundly asserted that, 'There is now direct visual evidence to show that, for centuries past, the British have had a continuing impulse to develop and enlarge, whenever the opportunity offered, certain kinds of freedom – particularly freedom of worship, freedom of government, and personal freedom.'[48] To this end all kinds of objects were displayed from gymslips to scythes in an attempt to show British life continuing undiverted by warfare from its immemorial origins to present times. This was the message Rowntree was to illustrate. It was undoubtedly painting by design and painting as design. The proportions were extraordinary, requiring a continuous

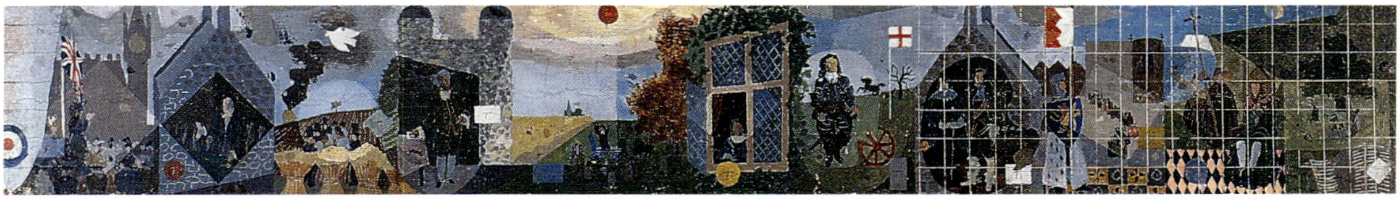

39 Study for the Freedom mural at the Festival of Britain 1951
Oil on card
10.2 x 71.8 cms (4 x 28.25 inches)

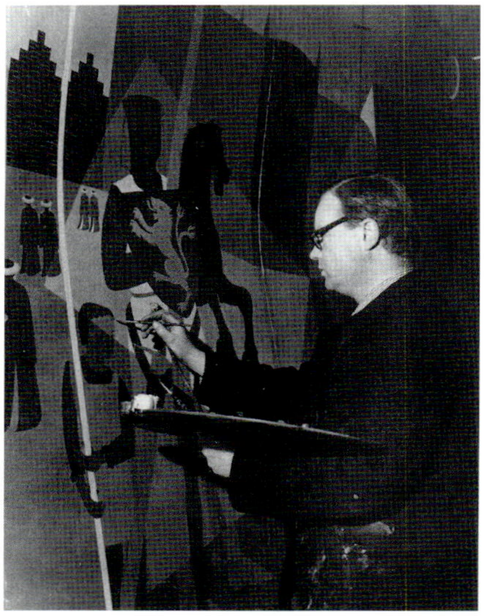

40 Kenneth Rowntree painting the *Freedom* mural in the Lion and Unicorn Pavilion at the Festival of Britain 1951
Photograph

narrative down the whole length. In this respect the earlier murals were an important precedent but so were the narrative sequences of his book covers. It called for the portrayal of a bright future when much of London's East End was still buried in rubble.[49] At the Festival of Britain historical themes constrained artistic experiment for Rowntree: it was difficult to reconcile artistic experimentation with a message of national endurance.[50]

In May 1951, Rowntree again showed work in Oxford at the *55th Exhibition of Pictures of the Oxford Art Society*, held in the Lower Gallery of the Ashmolean Museum. Rutherston's painting of a *Laundry Girl* was for sale at £157, whereas Rowntree's *Sussex Landscape with Factory Chimney* could be acquired for £31.

Comparable opportunities and restraints accompanied the coronation of Queen Elizabeth in 1953, although Rowntree's role did not stretch to murals. He made arrangements to paint events along the processional route. In a letter from the Ministry of Works, 25 March 1953, he learnt that, 'For a fee of £50 net you will paint some aspect of the coronation and let us have either two or three watercolour sketches or else one oil painting. As there is a possibility that we may want to reproduce the paintings in a publication the fee of £50 will include copyright.'[51] In due course the Queen acquired several works. *Last Minute Decorations* was exhibited in 1953 in a coronation exhibition along with works by other artists busy along the processional route that day, among them Edward Seago, Julian Trevelyan, Fred Uhlman, Carel Weight, Edward Bawden, Dame Laura Knight, Leonard Rosoman and Feliks Topolski.[52] About this time he even collaborated with John Skeaping RA to depict *Ballymoss and Scobie Breasley Winning the King George VI and Queen Elizabeth Stakes at Ascot*. It was the right moment for patriotic painting. Rowntree also decorated a coronation plate in gold along with a series of *Alphabet* jugs, and jugs decorated in a kind of black ground technique with stylised figures, that he had fired in the kilns at the Royal College of Art.

Not surprisingly there were more decorative commissions including murals for ships. The first of these, for RMS *Orcades*, was listed in the biographical note to the 1950 exhibition at the Leicester Galleries. In 1954 he made a mural for the first class dining room of the P. & O. Lines *Iberia* (Fig.41), for which a payment of £800 was agreed on 9 June 1954, the painting to be completed on five plywood panels. Rowntree proposed a cruise as part payment.[53]

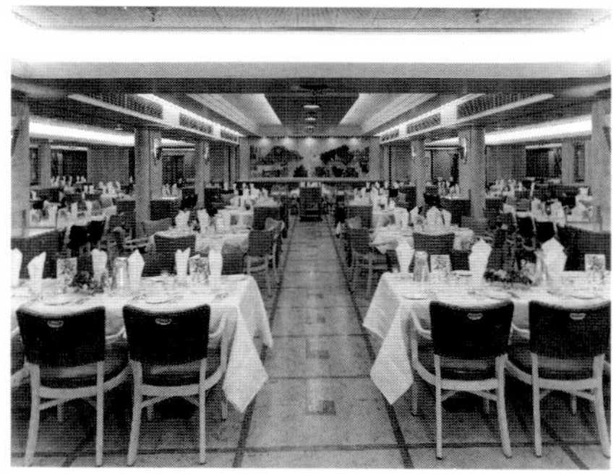

41 Mural painting on the liner RMS *Iberia* 1954
Photograph

Paintings for the Queen, the Festival of Britain and ocean-going liners suggested the possibility of future commissions. But Rowntree's paintings focused more upon personal experience than on public projects.

Open-Air Still-Life, Levisham (Fig.42) was painted in about 1954. Levisham and his aunt's holiday house there were a treasured part of his childhood. The still-life is itself intimate. The chair in the foreground has been vacated, perhaps by the painter. He has a place at the table (and so, by implication, has the viewer). The oil lamp on the table top establishes the still-life space, from which the two chairs already pull away. Beyond this, the nearby field reaches to the steep hillside. A drawing (Fig.43) reveals the editing skills by which he reduced the painting to its simplest elements. He eliminated a third chair and took the newspaper off the table, but retained the intricate lamp and emphasised the distant railway signal. From table and garden (home) to the distant hill and signal – is a measure of territory, from Levisham and the landscape of Yorkshire to the railway that connects with a bigger world. The Yorkshire identity had to be reconciled with metropolitan contacts to establish priorities. Meanwhile Diana too was addressing a world audience through architectural journalism in the *Manchester Guardian* newspaper.

Kenneth took care to exhibit in Yorkshire, at the *North Riding Artists' Exhibition*, for example, held in Scarborough Art Gallery (from 30 July to 28 August 1955), again with higher prices, including *Newtondale* for seventy-five guineas and an *Austrian Landscape* for forty guineas.[54] *Newtondale*'s price was the highest in the exhibition. He resubmitted it for the *Sixty-third Spring Exhibition of Modern British Paintings and Sculpture* at Bradford City Art Gallery, 16 March–27 May 1956, together with a *Landscape near Toulon*. This big exhibition (of 527 works) probably swamped his submissions. He gave his London address – 9 Ruvigny Gardens, SW15.

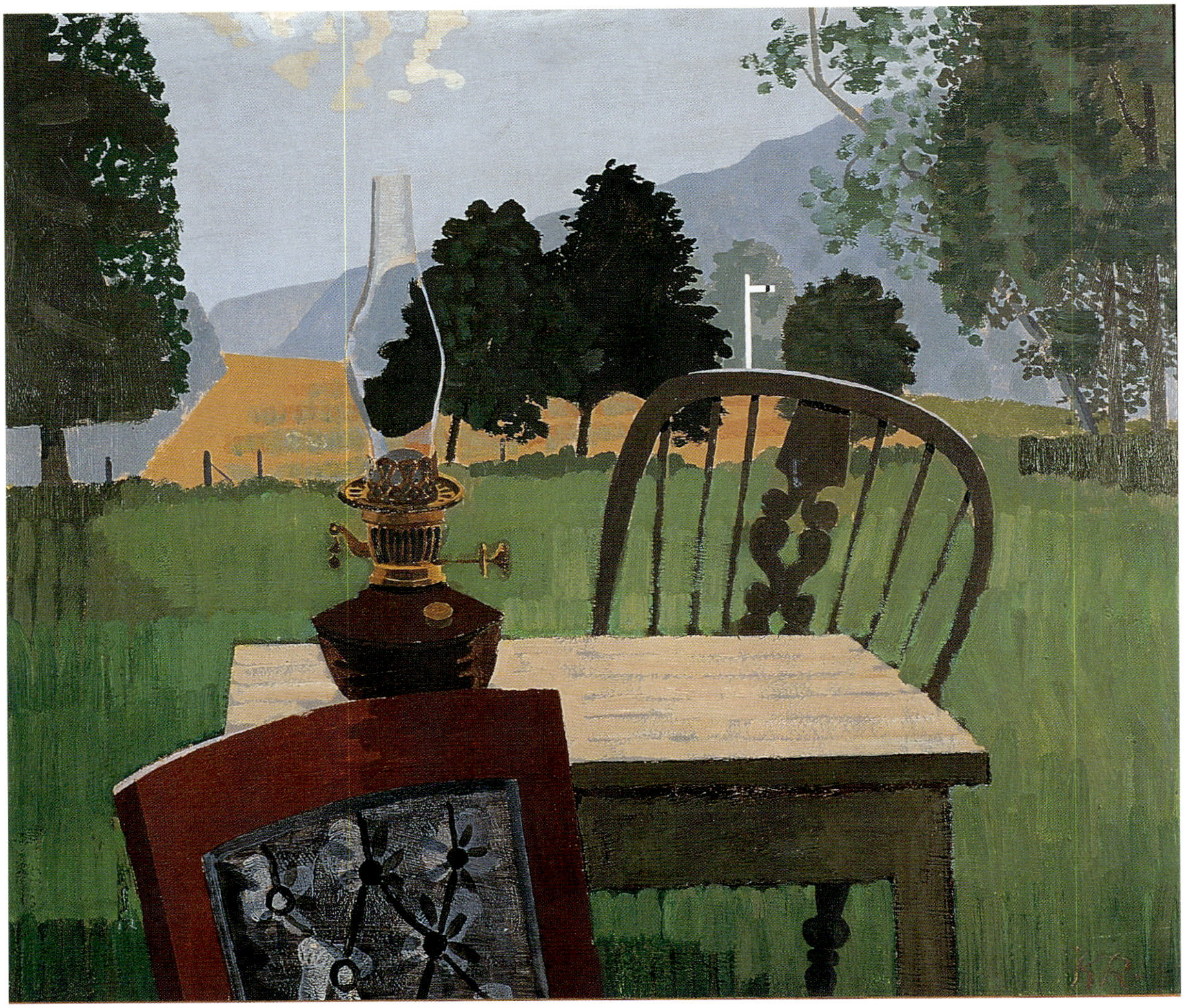

42 Open-Air Still-Life, Levisham 1954
Oil on board
78.7 x 91.5 cms (31 x 36 inches)

Ever since the *Swedish Still-Life*, Rowntree's love of the coast was evident. In *Holiday Bedroom, Little Haven (Pembrokeshire)* (Fig.44) the toy boat brings associations of the outside world of fresh air, movement and water into the house itself. The sea beyond the window is potentially more menacing. But boats of a very different kind occupied Rowntree in the mid 1950s. He turned again to Oxford, where almost heraldic simplification characterised his paintings of college barges, used as floating bases for spectators and rowers. The barges were in poor condition in 1956 when Diana Rowntree wrote about them in the *Architectural Review*.[55] They were 'disintegrating so fast that they may soon have disappeared altogether'.[56] She said that, 'Architecture, it is widely believed in Oxford, is a pursuit indistinguishable from stone'.[57] But she argued, 'this, no less than medieval stone, should be preserved'. After a history of Oxford barges since 1843, she pointed out that the boats were chosen because they were liked.[58] The article was thoroughly illustrated with drawings, photographs of barges and illustrations of the paintings (Fig.45).

These paintings were exhibited at the Ashmolean Museum in May 1956 in the building where Rowntree had studied as a youth. The *Manchester Guardian* declared them 'the fullest record possible of the gay if inconvenient settings of generations of oarsmen', attributing to the painter 'the exact combination of wit and poetry needed to convey the charm of these craft'.[59] He was seen as preserving the past, aware of a heritage that others took for granted. Some of the paintings sold, and three years later a further showing was arranged in the Memorial Room of Keble College, sponsored by the Boar Lane Gallery. The *Oxford Mail* declared that 'Posterity will have good cause to be grateful to Mr. Rowntree'.[60]

Yorkshire, Oxford, Essex, Wales, London – these were significant places, each with its role in his work. In each place he had celebrated the past visible in the present.[61] This theme had potential in work for tourism. He worked on the *Shell Guides* to Pembrokeshire, Lincolnshire and Yorkshire, and made a cover for Shell calendars celebrating England, Scotland and Wales. As local identity fascinated him, he was a good choice for these schemes. It also made him aware once more of the church as a focus of geography, history and identity. Church, chapel and cathedral were all painted with a Quaker's independence, but in each case stressing character in elevations, fittings and space, whether in St James, Piccadilly, a corrugated tin chapel or a vast cathedral.

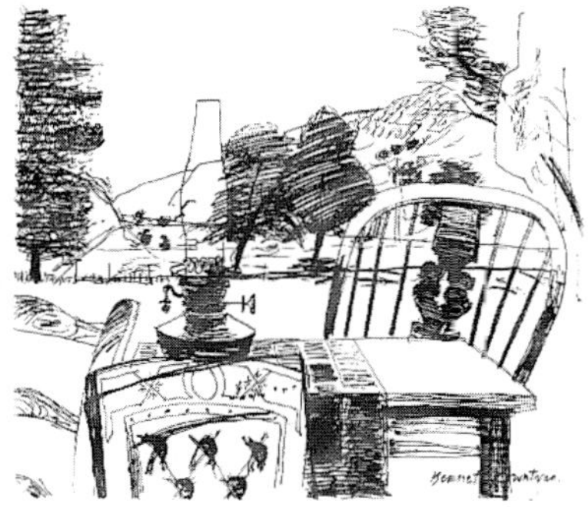

43 Open-Air Still-Life, Levisham 1954
Drawing on Paper; Signed lower right
40.7 x 50.8 cms (16 x 20 inches)

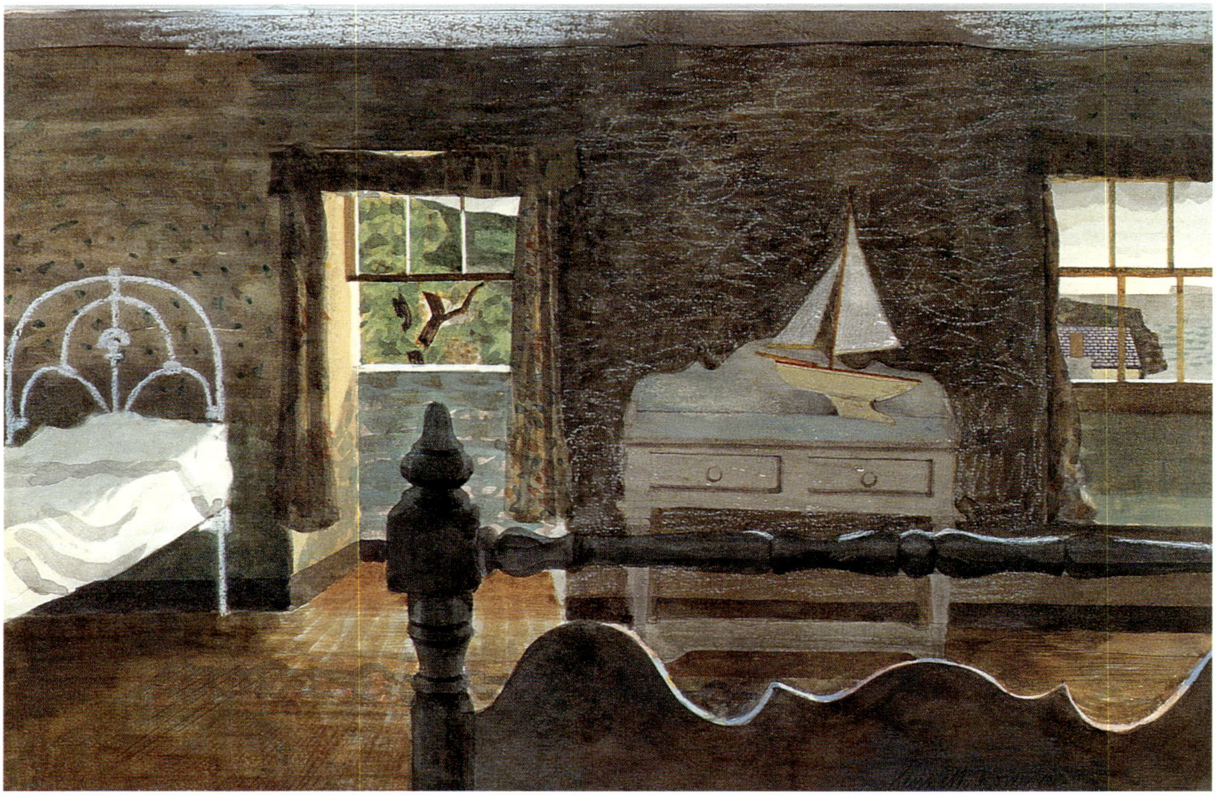

44 Holiday Bedroom, Little Haven (Pembrokeshire) *c.*1956
Watercolour on paper
54 x 69.3 cms (21.25 x 27.25 inches)

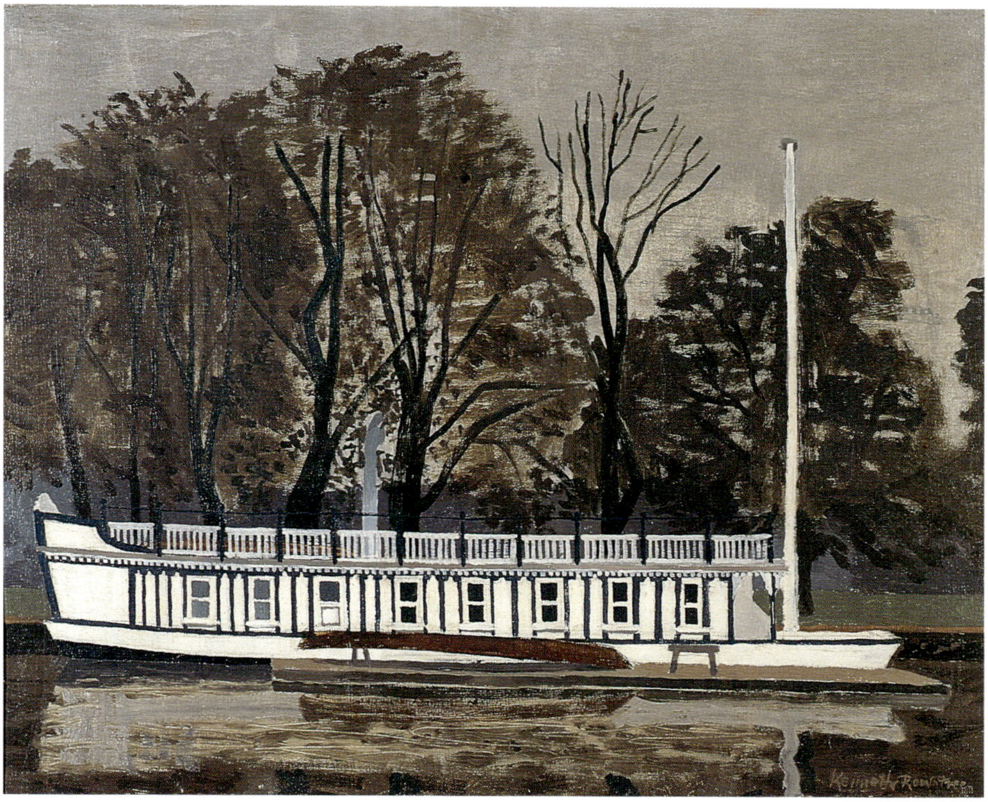

45 Lincoln College Barge, Oxford 1954
Oil on canvas
36.8 x 50.8 cms (14.5 x 20 inches)

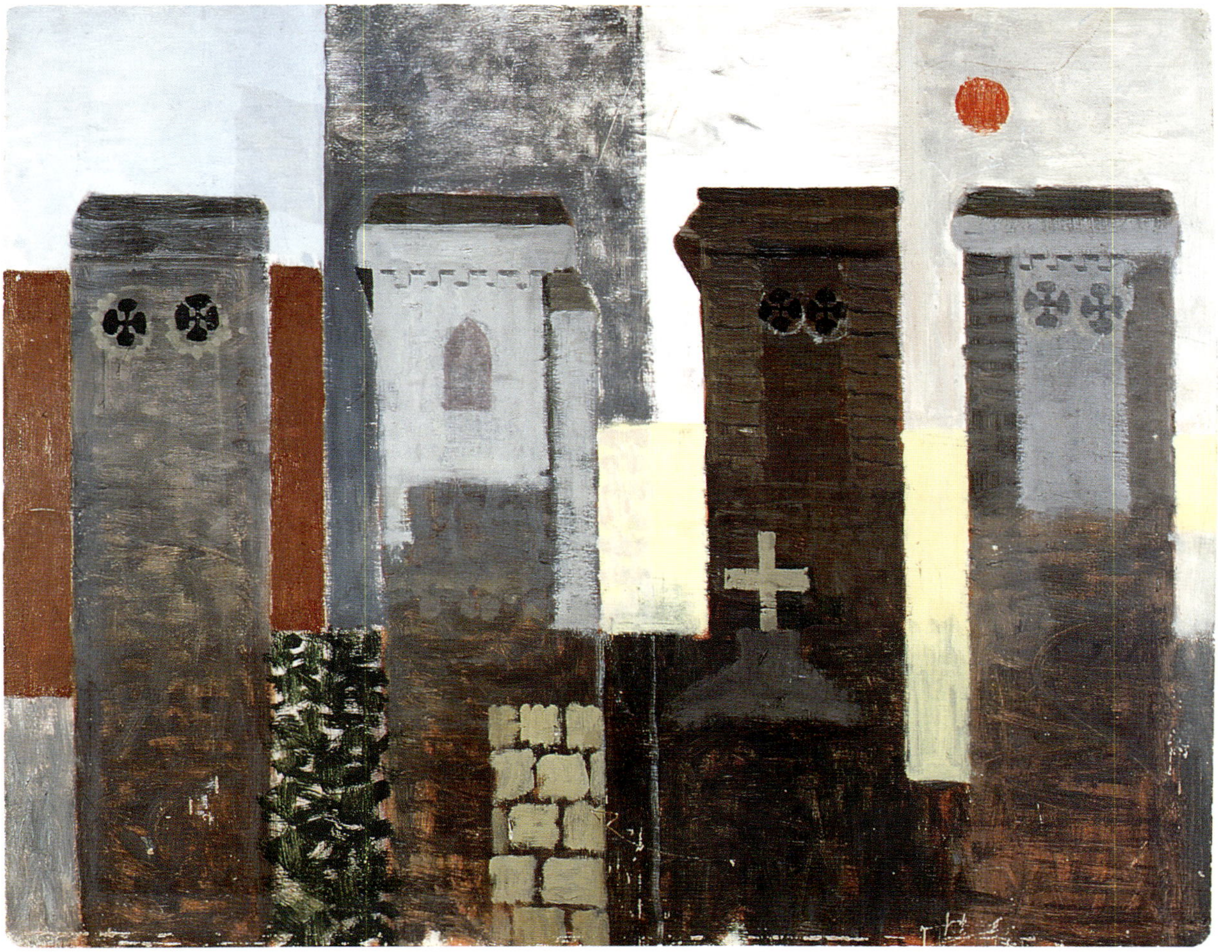

46 Malton Church, North Yorkshire
*c.*1954–6
Oil on board
71.2 x 91.5 cms (28 x 36 inches)

As postcard sellers know, great buildings are effective mementos of place. In *Malton Church, North Yorkshire* (Fig.46), painted about 1954–6, Rowntree isolated the church tower against the sky, assembling four elevations, one from each point of the compass, in four kinds of daylight as adjacent strips in one painting. He has given four moments that effectively emphasise the passage of time as the tower passes through darkness into daylight, its features catalogued across the composition.

Closer to the postcard images of isolated monumental grandeur were the paintings Rowntree made of Rheims Cathedral and Notre Dame. Rheims Cathedral dominates the canvas and the few small houses of the city visible at either side, asserting its role in the geography, history and identity of Rheims. The geometry of the elevation becomes the geometry of the painting. The power of *Rheims Cathedral in the Snow* (Fig.47) was matched in the brooding *Notre Dame* of the same year.

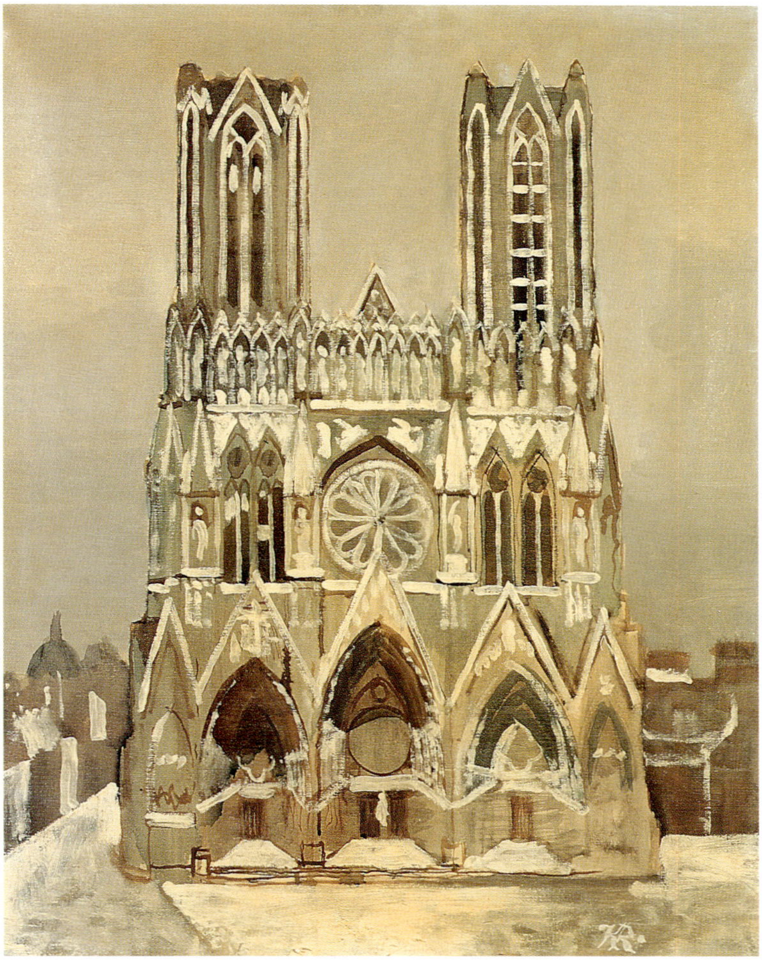

47 Rheims Cathedral in the Snow 1956
(also known as *Rheims in Snow*)
Oil on canvas
76.2 x 63.5 cms (30 x 25 inches)

The structure of this façade is transferred to canvas as the rhythms of a picture surface.

These paintings have a monumental quality by virtue of showing one vast object containing a myriad variations of geometry within it. The cathedral is a huge single still-life object, and in some paintings of this period Rowntree developed the open-air still-life format to contrast a foreground bottle, for example, with a distant cathedral tower, almost adjacent on the canvas surface.

IV Constructive Attitudes

In 1958 Rowntree's contract at the Royal College of Art ended. Robin Darwin, who had appointed him, wrote to thank him: 'My dear Kenneth this is just a note not of farewell, for I hope we shall never lose you altogether, but of thanks for all you have done in the Painting School and for the College as a whole for the last ten years.'[62]

Re-exhibiting the Oxford barge paintings was no substitute for a salary. But Rowntree's record was good and he soon found two significant appointments. He won a scholarship to paint in New Mexico and Nantucket. He also found a new post in a dynamic environment outside London. The Ford Foundation bursary to visit the United States came first.

Travel

On 8 April 1959 Rowntree was interviewed by the newspaper, the *New Orleans States and New Orleans Item*, under the headline 'Painter's delight: Britisher loves our cemeteries'. The journalist Bob Friendly quoted Rowntree, '"Sounds rather ghoulish but I love them", he commented as he left the DeSoto hotel with water colors, five brushes, a water flask, collapsible seat and the kitchen plate he uses as an easel *[sic]*. "There is great aesthetic pleasure for me in the cut lettering on tombstones," the graying middle-aged redhead pointed out. "Cemeteries are very good to paint."'[63] After New Orleans, he moved to Santa Fe, New Mexico, before heading north to New York, Nantucket and Boston.

The new landscapes and cultures of America refreshed him after so long a study of the landscapes, buildings and traditions of Britain. In New Mexico especially, he produced works of startling originality and brilliant colour, adapting old strategies to deal with intense light and

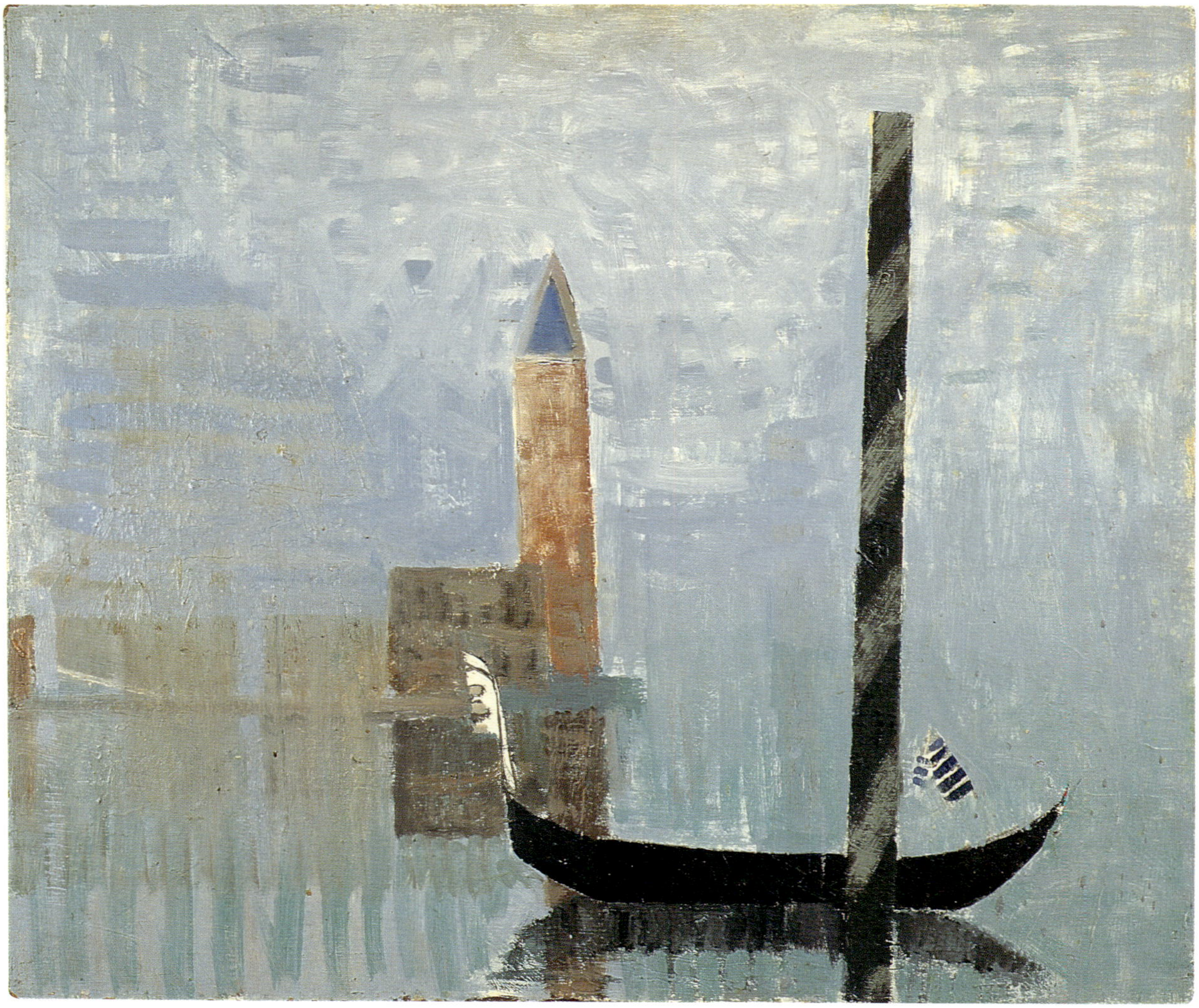

48 Venice, dawn 1960
Oil on board
63.5 x 76.2 cms (25 x 30 inches)

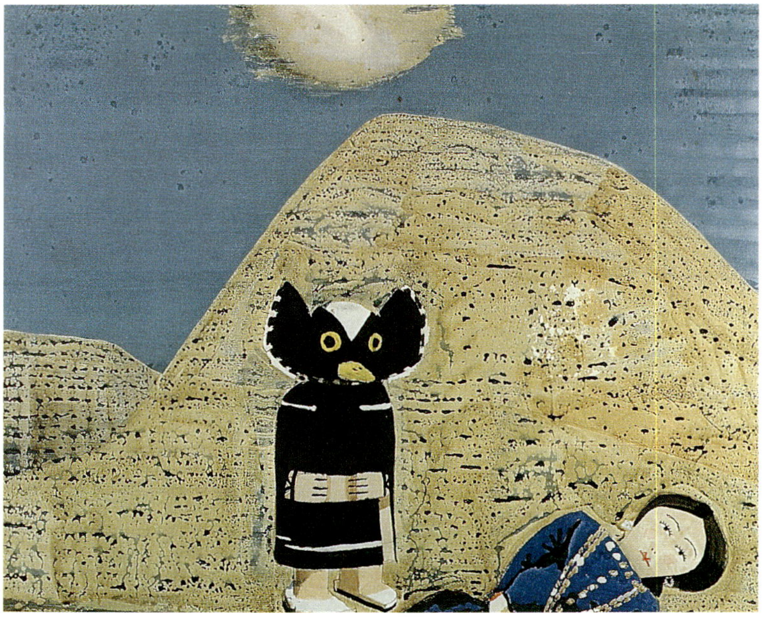

49 New Mexico Encounter (Katchina and Mexican Dolls) 1959
Watercolour on paper
48.3 x 61 cms (19 x 24 inches)
Hatton Gallery, University of Newcastle

new imagery. *New Mexico Encounter (Katchina and Mexican Dolls)* (Fig.49) is a radical painting in its powerful light, strong colour, elemental composition and extraordinary subject. Out of only five elements (sky, cloud, hills, two dolls) he created an intense drama. The hillside was painted with wax so that the sky's blue would not adhere to it but other paint was scumbled in to dry in the small globules that texture the landscape. The dolls have strong, assertive accents of black and blue. The effect is to make inanimate objects look alive. Painted with great freshness, direct techniques and a minimum of elements, this makes a powerful work.

He also portrayed the Deep South in watercolours[64] and in a collage project intended for *Vogue* magazine. Here the motif of travel itself is made clear with tickets applied to the gouache landscape. Place in these collages has become destination. This is equally so in *Nantucket* (Fig.50), his northern counterpart to the heat of the South. Even here there are characteristic motifs of church towers. A whole series of paintings followed from the studies of Nantucket in the whale-fishing regions of the North. The placing of elements had a profound effect, whether geometric (a gable-end or road sign), a pattern (the stripes on a lighthouse) or natural (small, broken clouds across the sky).[65]

These rhythmic clouds call to mind the work of Victor Pasmore, but this was Rowntree's spontaneous invention which was not yet visible in Pasmore's work. He had exhibited with Pasmore more than once and saw *Waterfall*, Pasmore's ceramic mural of spiralling and tumbling curves applied to the exterior of the Regatta restaurant at the Festival of Britain. Rowntree's work was atmospheric in its vision of the rhythm of clouds. To Rowntree at this point, Pasmore's move from representation may well have appeared simply architectural decoration. As the *New Orleans States and New Orleans Item* had commented: 'Rowntree had a good word for contemporary abstract painters, though he does not claim to be one. He finds that his own work is "moving towards abstraction".' It went on to quote Rowntree: '"There is good abstract art and there is bad, just as in any of the other forms .... Abstract art is a matter of simplification ... discarding things that are not necessary."'[66]

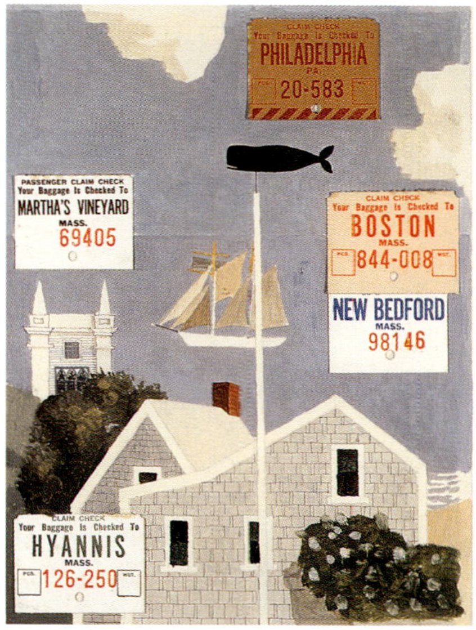

50 Nantucket 1959–60
Projected design for *Vogue*
Oil and collage on card
33 x 24.2 cms (13 x 9.5 inches)

Rowntree still exhibited with Oxford and London associates for whom the recognisable image was important. In June–July 1959 in Oxford, for example, fellow exhibitors included Gilbert and Stanley Spencer, Graham Sutherland, John Piper, John Nash, Paul Nash, William Orpen and John Minton as well as Albert Rutherston, Randolph Schwabe and Barnett Freedman.[67] This was also true of the exhibition to which Rowntree contributed at the New Art Centre in London in 1959.

Newcastle

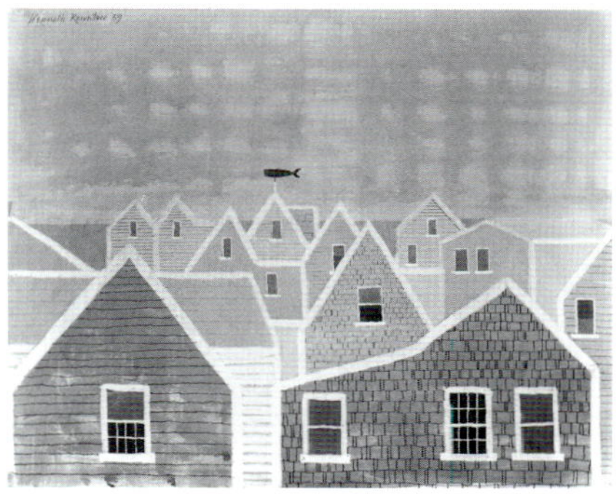

51 Nantucket I 1959
Watercolour on paper
48.4 x 61 cms (19 x 24 inches)
Collection Mr and Mrs Medd

In the new appointment, taken up on his return from the United States, Rowntree might have expected a quiet life at a provincial art school, but nothing could have been further from the truth. On becoming Professor at the Department of Fine Art in Durham University at Newcastle he had entered an environment that was to transform his art. Lawrence Gowing was the departing professor and the staff included Quentin Bell (a contender for the post), Victor Pasmore and Richard Hamilton. The last two, together and separately, were engaged in a creative dialogue that changed aspects of British art, art education and exhibition curation almost out of all recognition.

Pasmore's transformation into a radical experimental artist had been hastened by his discovery of Charles Biederman's *Art as the Evolution of Visual Knowledge*, first published in 1948, a book he was studying by 1951. Its preference for 'structural factors' over 'fantasy factors' was a sustained promotion of the international Constructive art movements of the 1920s and 1930s which in England had their effect on Ben Nicholson and others, ensuring a welcome for Naum Gabo and for Mondrian just before the war.[68] Nor was Pasmore alone; the Artists'

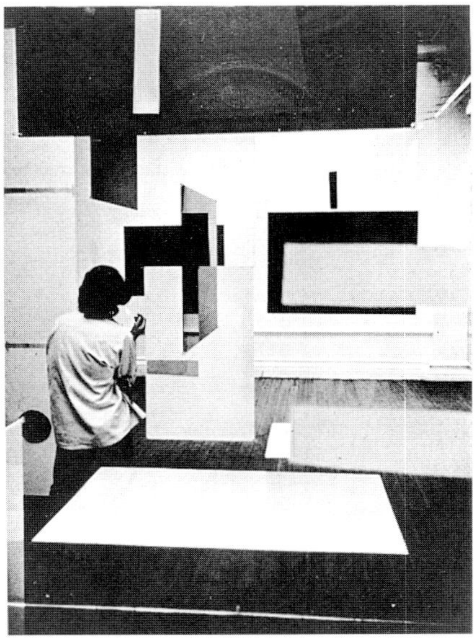

52 Victor Pasmore and Richard Hamilton
A spatial construction at the installation
An Exhibit, Hatton Gallery 1957
Acrylic sheets and nylon thread
Photograph Richard Hamilton

International Association (AIA) in London, for example, published *Broadsheet No. 1*, devoted to abstract art, in 1951.[69]

Another influential book received special attention that year. D'Arcy Thompson's *Growth and Form*[70] considered natural structures in plants and crystals. *Growth and Form* was also the title adopted by Richard Hamilton for his first major installation and curatorial project held at the Institute of Contemporary Arts (ICA) in London in 1951. Hamilton and Pasmore both approached visual creativity as an investigation.

Richard Hamilton taught in Newcastle from 1953, alongside Gowing, Quentin Bell and the art historian Ralph Holland. Gowing was already a trustee of the Tate Gallery. This alignment comprised a rich mixture of art, curating, theory, art history and writing. Hamilton contributed to all of these areas, adding also his expertise as a designer. Pasmore moved to Newcastle in 1954, and put on *Abstract Art* that year, including work by Hepworth, Kenneth and Mary Martin, and Ben Nicholson alongside his own relief constructions.

The next year Hamilton launched *Man, Machine and Motion* at the Hatton Gallery, comprising melamine panels on which were printed photographic and popular images of human interaction with machines in motion. Its structure within the gallery was comparable to Pasmore's systematic construction of reliefs, a process using proportional systems that he described in *Art News* in 1956 in an interview with Lawrence Alloway.[71] Collaborating with Hamilton, Pasmore made *An Exhibit*, installed in the Hatton Gallery (Fig.52), and later at the ICA in June 1957.[72] Alloway wrote the catalogue essay. This was the challenging environment into which Rowntree stepped.

Hamilton staged an exhibition of The Independent Group in 1958,[73] and Pasmore was exhibiting *Basic Forms*.[74] Hamilton designed the catalogue for *The Developing Process* at the Hatton Gallery. The exhibition and the teaching were part of a single Constructive approach.[75] The catalogue acknowledged the influence of the Bauhaus Basic Course (*Vorkurs*), and declared 'We no longer think of painting as the property of a cultural élite, but as a means of visual communication with its own particular characteristics existing in a communications continuum.'[76] Pasmore sought 'the development of new foundations in art training, on a scientific basis, suitable for introduction into schools of art and technology' as being 'a necessary step following upon the decline of the classical academies.'[77] Hamilton set his students tasks 'designed to allow only a reasoned result.'[78]

The studios were filling up with Constructive works when Rowntree arrived. Pasmore's innovations were at their height and Hamilton immaculately designed the catalogue of the Pasmore exhibition at the Hatton Gallery in 1960.[79] Pasmore showed at the Venice Biennale while Hamilton continued his prolific investigations and publications. Meanwhile the Hatton Gallery had major exhibitions including *Schwitters* (1959) and *The Estorick Collection* with works by Picasso, Braque and Gris as well as Ben Nicholson.[80]

A new departure or Rowntree's response

Rowntree's response to this tumultuous invention, ambition and talent, was to engage in a vigorous creative dialogue that never undermined his original identity. *Putney Landscape* of 1960 is both geometric and representational, as are *Studio Window and Putney Reach* (Fig.53). A watercolour, *Putney Boats*, could be construed as a relief. This was a new way of working with little apparent room for signs of memory or personality. But Rowntree put back these qualities with visual puns, specific references and surprises, bringing irreverent wit to Constructive art.

He developed sequences of works on a single theme permitting the viewer to trace the variations. *Venice, dawn* (Fig.48) is filled with a limpid, wet and misty atmosphere in which a gondolier passes the bell tower of St Mark's. There are visual rhymes of striped jersey and striped pole, but mostly the geometric aspect is subsidiary to the light and incident. The Tate Gallery's *Souvenir of Venice* (Fig.54) is bigger and more fully resolved with rich colour and textured surfaces contrasting with the ball/sun, and lines too ambiguous to interpret, seen against the sky. Variations proliferated as invention replaced observation. *Black Painting* (Fig.55) of 1961 shows that he was willing to take the theme beyond recognition. The 'cue' motif has dislocated all the pictorial elements into the simplest dynamic and geometric forms.

Three variations called *Shapes in Movement II* (Fig.56) followed *Black Painting*. Their perspex upper surface has another layer below so that changes appear as the viewer moves. *Shapes on Blue II* (Fig.57) finally relinquished the triangle motif, but retained the 'cue' motif.[81] A final variation was constructed in perspex, a specific response to the demand to use synthetic materials.[82] Here the variation is almost independent of its theme. Structurally close to Pasmore's work, its wit is wholly

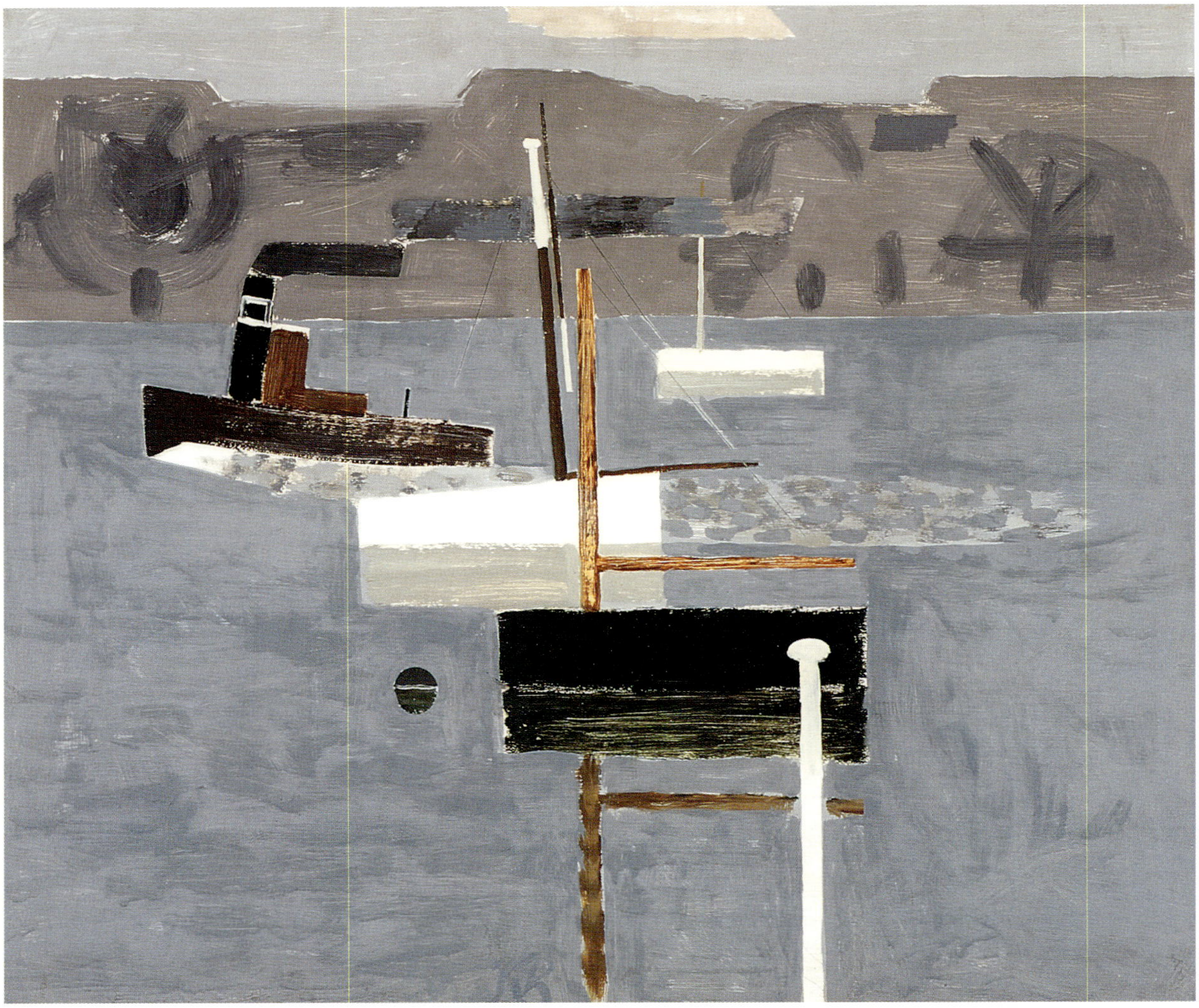

53 Putney Reach 1960
Oil on gesso on board
63 x 75 cms (24.75 x 29.5 inches)

Rowntree's. This was an intellectual and creative dialogue more radical than the Royal College provided. It was a game that Rowntree played his own way, adding an edge of irony that delighted him. Pasmore left Newcastle in 1961 to pursue his independent career, but Rowntree also exhibited in London, showing his latest work at the Zwemmer Gallery in 1962.[83] He was not doctrinaire however: he included fifteen American watercolours alongside geometric works, paintings from either side of the debate over representation. His work thrived between the two, but it was not an easy position to sustain.

Translations of buildings into geometric constructions followed as a natural development of long standing interests. *Aberdovey*, painted about 1963, has the black background of *Black Painting* with towers and triangular roofs. Two gable-ends, one shallow and yellow, one steep and white, rear up between them. In front of these is the suggestion of a

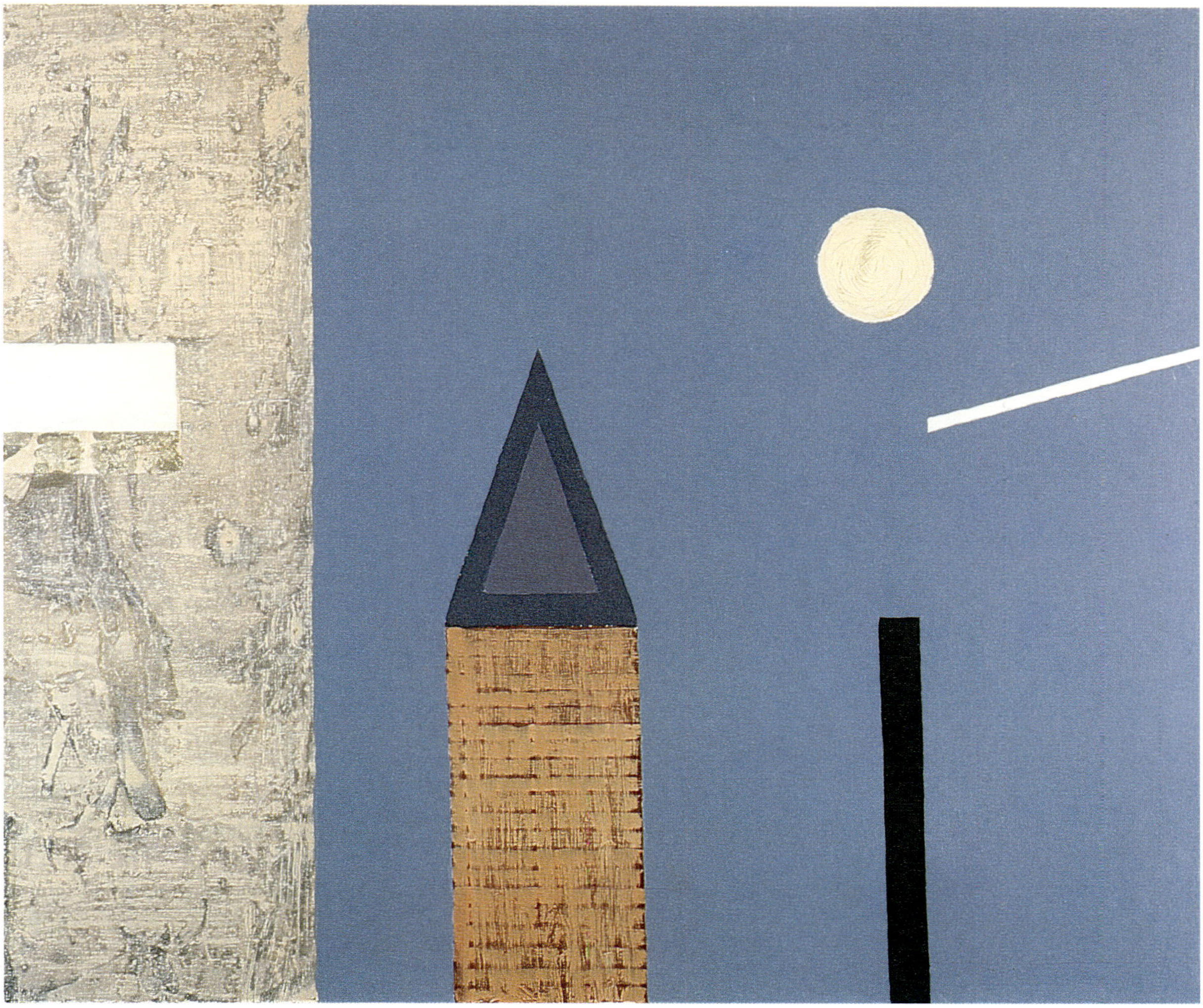

54 Souvenir of Venice 1961
Oil on board
63.5 x 76.2 cms (25 x 35 inches)
The Tate Gallery, London (T03935)
Presented by the Friends of the Tate Gallery 1984

black roof and a striped coffee mug on a windowsill. This replays earlier themes in a Welsh context including the format of foreground still-life motif (striped mug). At left, the curved form of a tree is visible, its shape like the form in *Shapes on Blue II* (Fig.57), with the 'cue' motif visible at right. The cross above in a perspective plane, has a radiant effect perhaps representing a light. He was playing off themes and motifs in a complex composition determined to establish the point where the images are lost and the geometry of shapes predominates.

The same techniques with new elements produced the black painting called *Putney Bridge, Nightpiece*. Spots and stripes together mark lamps on the bridge reflected in the Thames, with a bus crossing over and warning lights for the river traffic. Three textures of black paint achieve the main composition and its atmosphere of urban night. The nocturne, surprisingly, recalls Whistler's, night paintings.

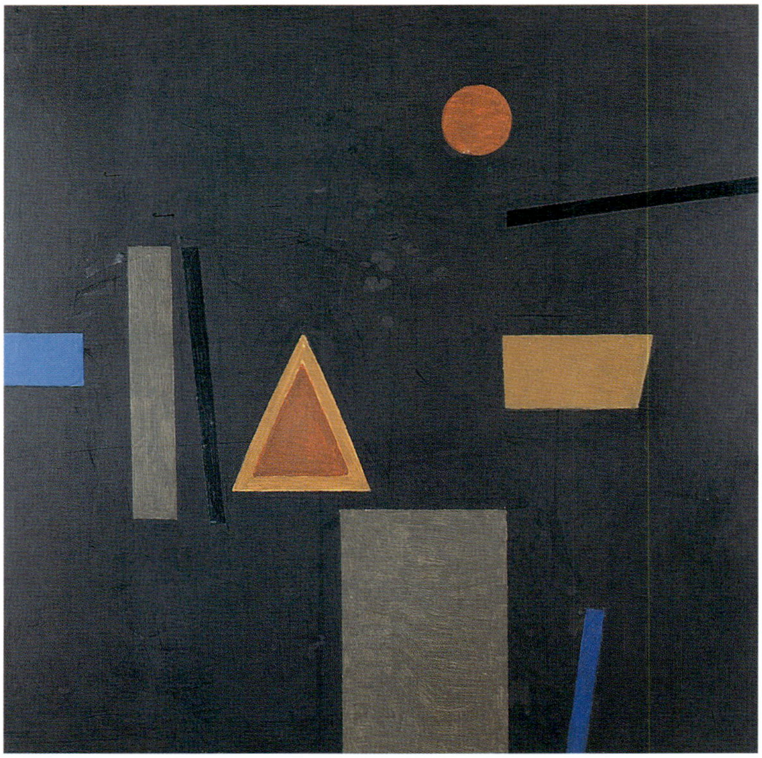

55 Black Painting 1961
(also known as *Black Painting, Venice* and *Venice Painting*)
Oil on board
58.5 x 61 cms (23 x 24 inches)

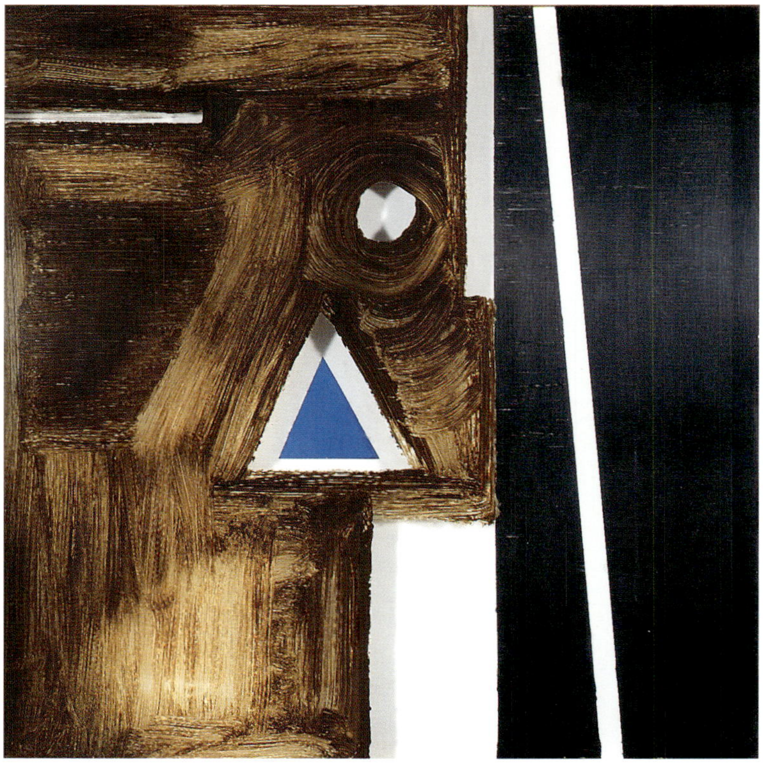

56 Shapes in Movement II 1960
Oil on perspex reversed
53.4 x 53.4 cms (21 x 21 inches)

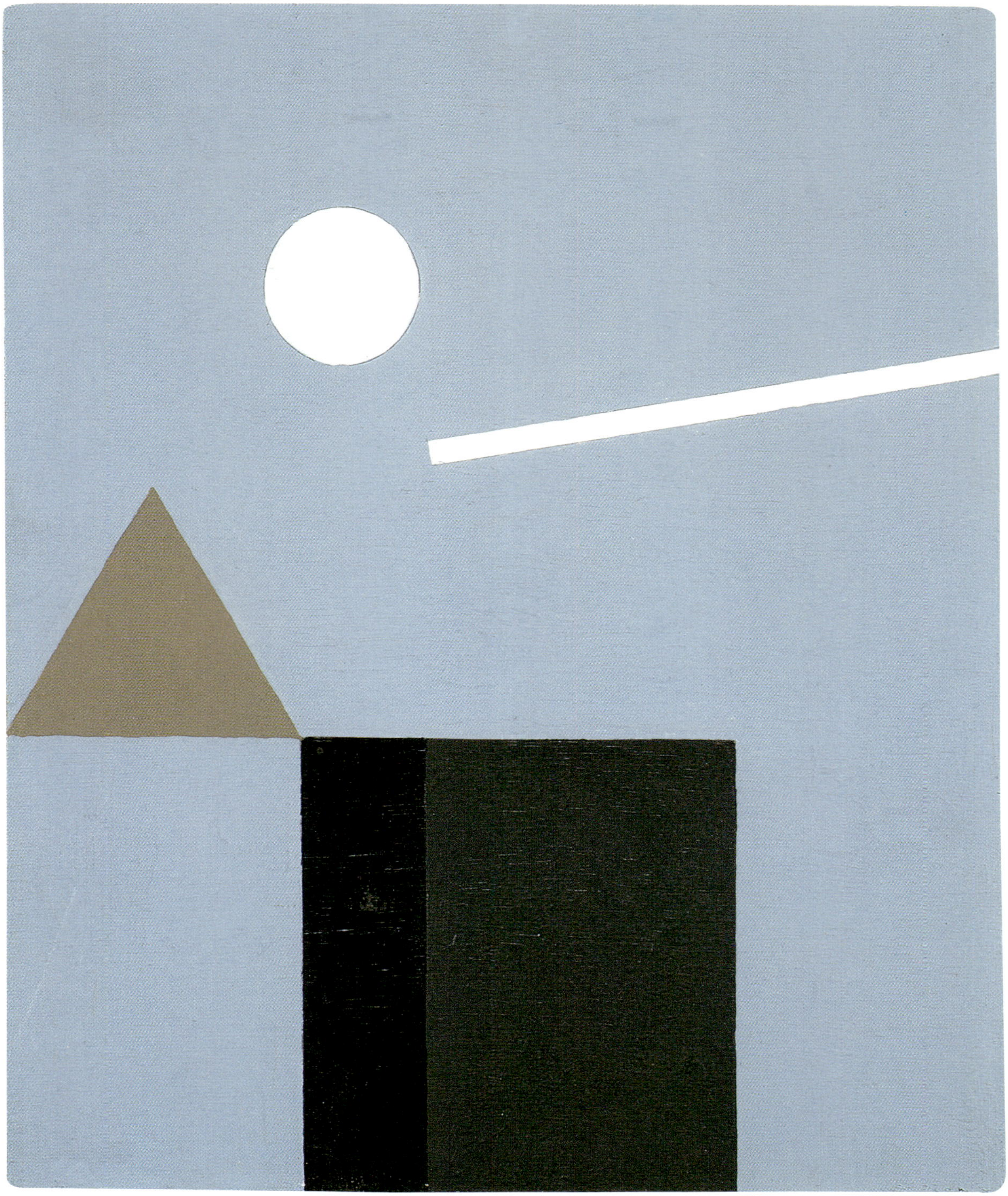

57 Shapes on Blue II 1961
Oil on board
40.6 x 50.8 cms (16 x 20 inches)

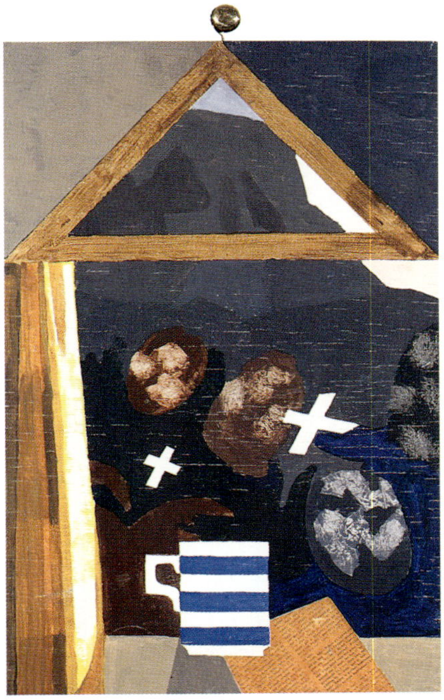

58 Welsh Attic Window 1963
Oil and collage on board, brass knob
56.5 x 38.1 cms (22.25 x 15 inches)

Aberdovey motifs recur in *Welsh Attic Window* (Fig.58), a work which is daylit and colourful. The blue-striped jug is easily recognised on its windowsill with trees and a craggy hillside outside. The big triangle is now a dormer window. Above it a real brass knob connects the painting to the wall.[84] These paintings are still views of landscape, windows through which the viewer may look. Occasionally the full freshness of 'painting a view' returns in the midst of all of Rowntree's experiments. *Italian Landscape* (Fig.59) of 1964 is a case of this. Severely edited and rhythmically structured, it nevertheless has the wide space, fresco colour and grand calm of Piero della Francesca.

Design and Dada

The Basic Course at Newcastle sought to bring together art and design. Painting as structured, edited and controlled as this, has a designed aspect to it and begins to suggest a wall and a room in which to house it. Kenneth and Diana designed interiors with such skill that even the view through the window seemed an intended pictorial effect. An explanation of such practical and visual organisation was provided by Diana when Penguin Books published *Interior Design* in 1964. It remains a useful and persuasive book. She asserted that a room is neither a painting nor a sculpture, but a space inside a solid. She gave illustrations of fine, clear and modern interiors. The continuum of construction, from architecture to painting and back, was a well-established route by 1964. Pasmore, after all, had worked on housing at Peterlee in County Durham. Diana also used a photograph of Richard Hamilton's studio in Highgate.

Hamilton at the time was investigating anti-art and Dada. He published a typographic version of Marcel Duchamp's *Green Box* in 1960[85] related to his study of Duchamp's *Bride Stripped Bare by her Bachelors, even*, which addressed the image of the figure as a mechanised sexual creature, a theme used also by the Dadaist Francis Picabia in works exhibited at the Hatton Gallery in 1964, with a catalogue constructed faultlessly by Hamilton and an essay by Ron Hunt. *Voilà la Femme* (Here is Woman) by Picabia depicted a rudimentary engine with pistons. *Femme au Miroir* (Woman at the Mirror) showed a disappearing figure of silhouettes, profiles and reflections. These Dadaists were studied intensely at Newcastle in the 1960s, when Rowntree too was working on the figure motif. There is, for example, in *Flowers Girl/Girl Flowers* (Fig.60), a portrait with the face obscured by flowers.

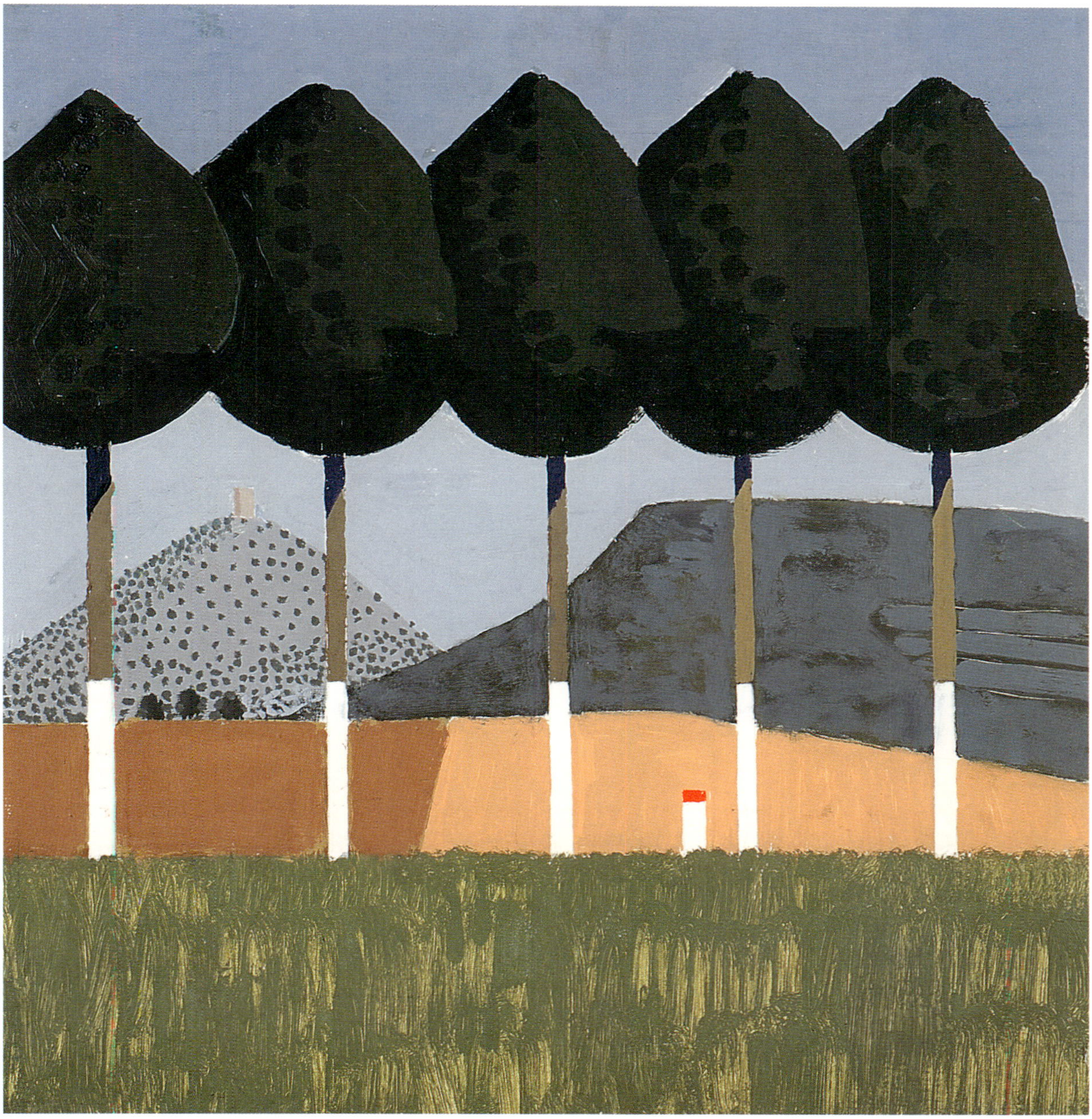

59 Italian Landscape 1964
Acrylic paint on board
76.2 x 76.2 cms (30 x 30 inches)

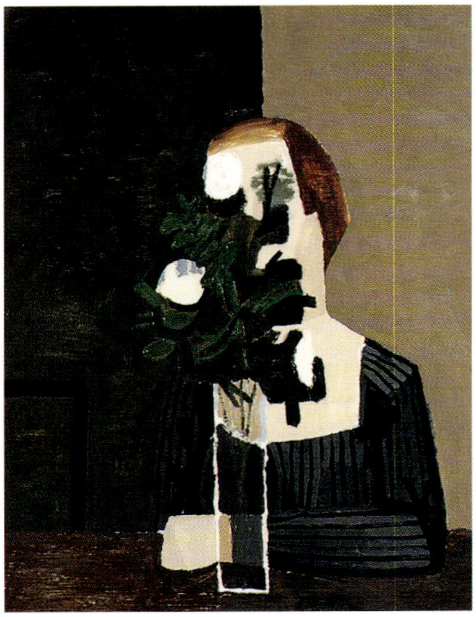

60 Flowers Girl/Girl Flowers 1963
Oil on board
99.1 x 83.8 cms (39 x 33 inches)

Even more extraordinary was the series of paintings, horizontal in format with four to eight sections, representing figures. *Fourfigure II* (Fig.61) was exhibited at the New Art Centre, London, in 1970. Each rectangle is a single colour, or striped, and one has a hemispherical form to represent a breast. A screenprint variant, called *Welsh Print* (Tate Gallery) has six sections or three figures, one decorated with Welsh language newspaper. The stylised images of the *Vogue* project form a useful comparison. As there, so here, the figure is fleeting, anonymous and mysterious, yet the attributes that we do see are simple, elegant, informal and stylish. The series included a three-figure painting and several *Twofigure* relief paintings where the front view includes the circular breast motif, and indications of pockets on the back view. In one case the female front view has the forward movement of a thigh beneath the skirt. These fragmentary presences have youth, style and sensuality.

Breton Morning (Fig.62) of 1965 took the series one step further. The figure at left has a blue skirt and black top with a breast indicated. Beyond a white table stretches a field of brown beneath a paler sky and a heavy curving cloud. Such a language of signs is no more extreme than *African figures* or Duchamp's *Bride*. Both featured in the Hatton Gallery in 1966, though Duchamp's *Bride Stripped bare by her Bachelors, even*, was presented in Hamilton's meticulous and scholarly reconstruction (Tate Gallery) entitled *The Bride Stripped bare by her Bachelors even, again*.

Single figures flowed from Rowntree's studio in blue and white, a breast indicated and a leg stepping forward beneath the skirt (Fig.63). Signs mark a head, and breasts, arms and skirt. A colour scheme especially emphasising blue and white, the stillness of the girl, even now distantly recalls Vermeer, though the differences far outweigh any similarities.

Rowntree's department acquired harmonious and extensive new buildings by Sheppard and Robson in 1968, and was now known internationally.

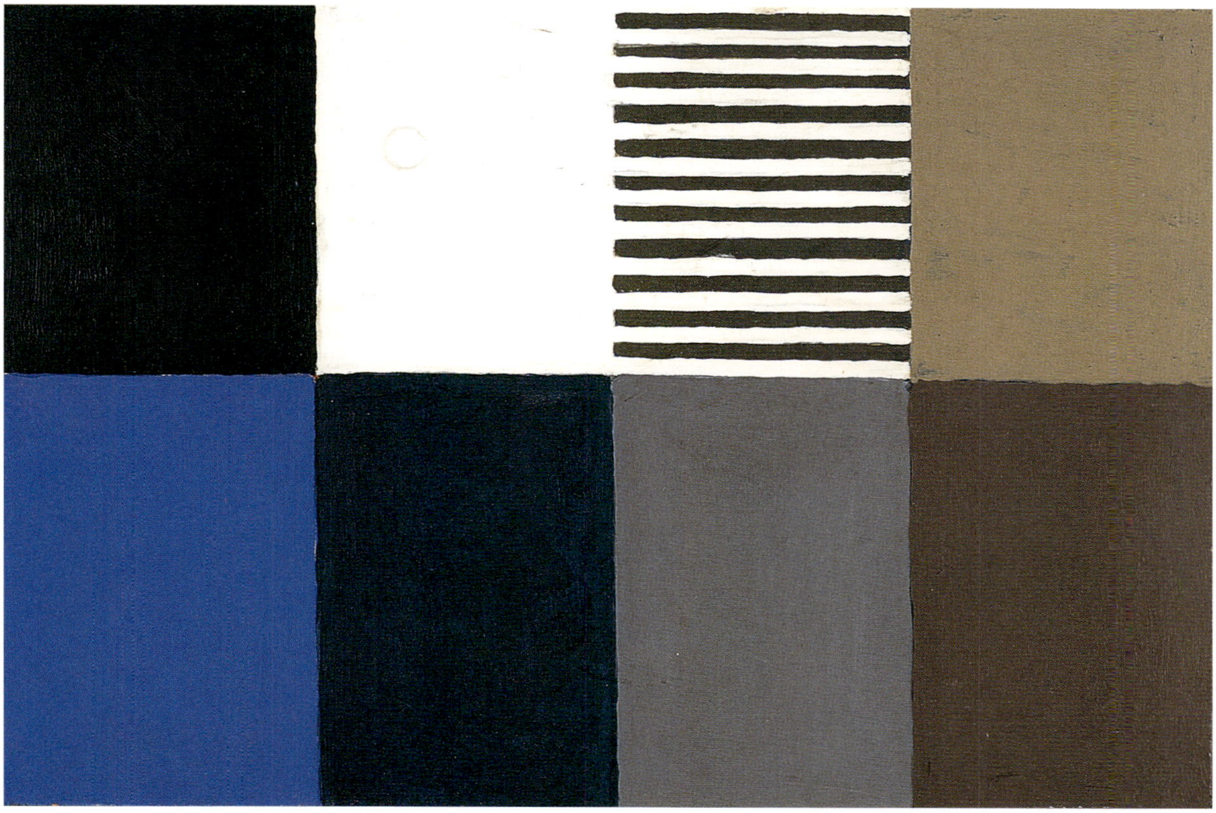

61 Fourfigure II 1964
Acrylic paint on board
20.4 x 30.5 cms (8 x 12 inches)

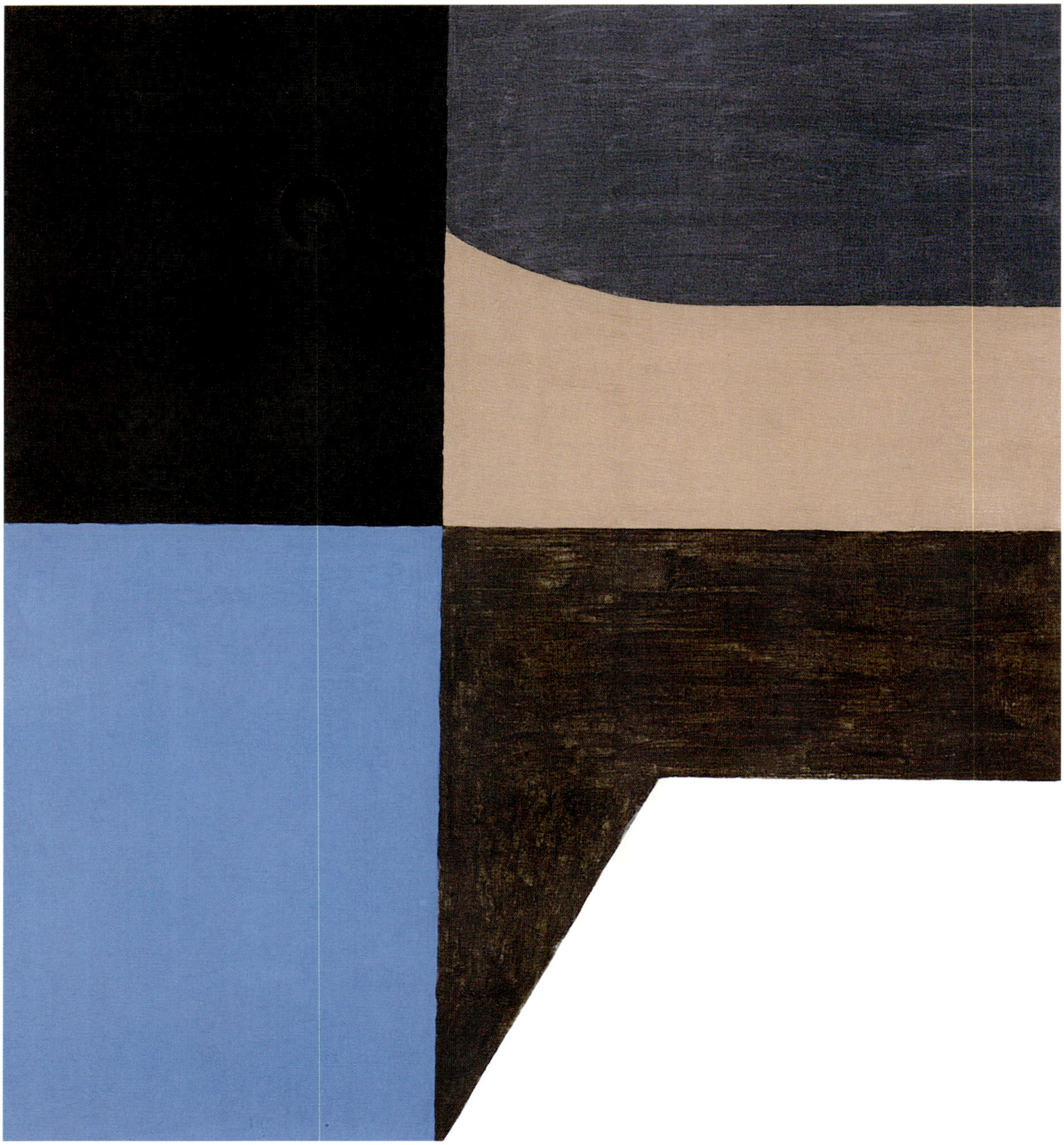

62 Breton Morning 1965
Acrylic paint on board
61 x 55.9 cms (24 x 22 inches)

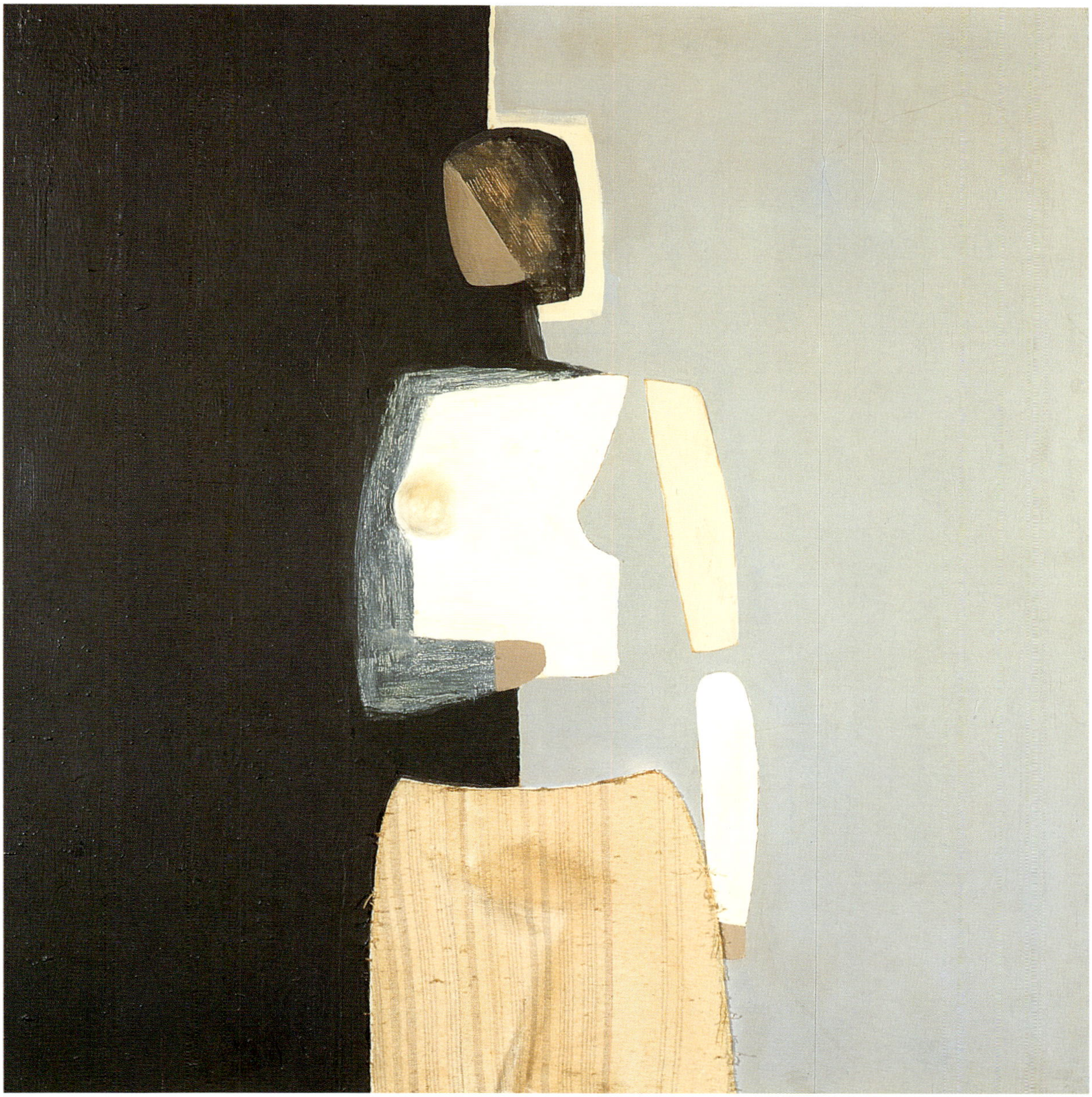

63 Girl in Five Parts 1967–8
Acrylic paint on board
61 x 61 cms (24 x 24 inches)

V Later Work

When Rowntree was able to consolidate his achievements he made a rediscovery of lettering and typography.

Voiture 35 (Fig.64) is a collage that is atmospheric and suggestive. It fits Mallarmé's idea that poetry should not spell out its message but draw in the viewer with clues to complete it in an act of imagination.

Voiture 35 (Car 35) suggests a French railway carriage. The printed notice is simply pasted onto the collage with all its typographic qualities intact. The horizontal pale line may be a window guard with a sunshade device: *Voiture 35* appears to be pasted on a window looking out onto dry, textured hills. The clues evoke a carriage moving smoothly past the mountains of southern France. He was now working with acrylic paint which dried fast, could act as a glue, and easily made flat surfaces of colour. His friend, the painter Sidney Nolan, may have introduced him to the medium. Water-based and matt in surface, it unites many of the possibilities of watercolour and oil paint.

Rowntree had not abandoned relief constructions however, many of which now involved no paint at all but incorporated words, reflecting his interest in concrete poetry in which the spatial and material aspects of lettering were often important. The cubist poet Apollinaire (1880–1918) had made shaped poems and Rowntree may refer to Apollinaire in his collage *Verres et alcool* (Glasses and Alcohol) (Fig.65) in 1969.[86] This construction in acrylic paint, wood, perspex, paper and cloth is an open-air still-life with the Pyrenees rising behind the boxes. The mountains at left are made from a page of a French telephone directory. The bold type of the names gives weight to the lower slopes, whilst the lighter type of the addresses reaches up to the peaks where the white page transforms visually into snow. Like concrete poetry, this relief uses analogy and metaphor, subverting one material, word and idea into another.

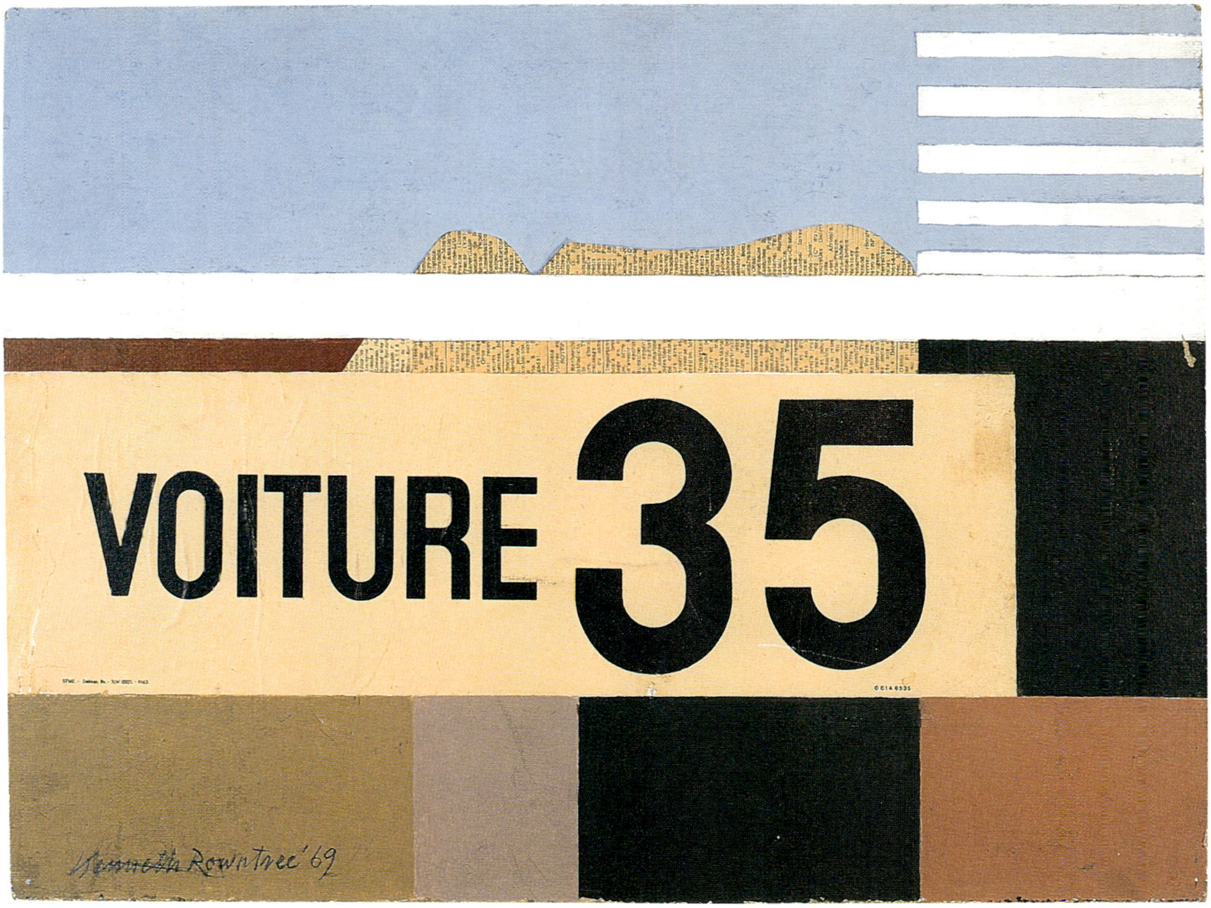

64 Voiture 35 1969
Acrylic paint and paper collage
37 x 50 cms (14.5 x 19.75 inches)

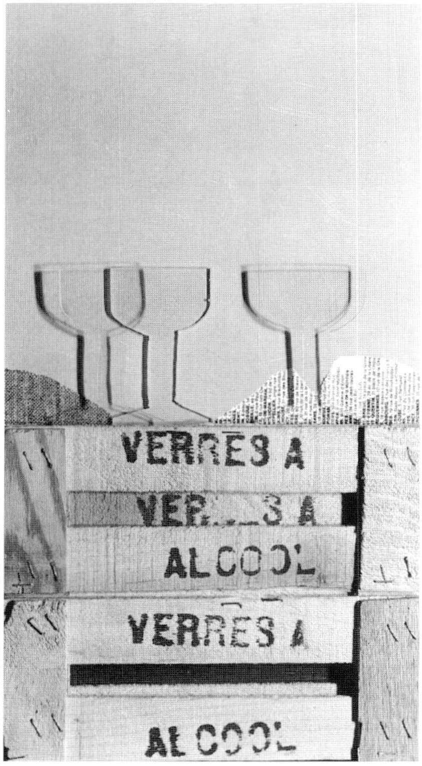

65 Verres et alcool 1969
Acrylic paint, wood, perspex
33.7 x 18.4 cms (13.25 x 7.25 inches)

Kenneth travelled to the Pyrenees in 1968 to stay with Marghanita Laski at Les Forges de Montgaillard. The collage *Foothills of the Pyrenees* (Fig.66) of 1969 uses only newsprint and tickets to make the fields and geology of the mountains. *Coffee-pot, cup, table: The Pyrenees* uses paper, wood, cloth, silver paper, perspex and paint on board, as does *Bottle, Glass, Table: The Pyrenees* (Fig.67). These are minimal relief constructions, sometimes using cubist devices of collage and transparency, but so rich in textural contrasts and other material qualities that the absence of paint is scarcely noticed. Found materials transform into depictions of other objects, in a metamorphosis with its own strange blend of realism and illusion. For *Cup in a Landscape* of 1970, Rowntree sawed a cup in half to sit it on a fragment of wood for the table top. As a result, the half-cup convincingly represents the whole cup, as it would in a painting.

By this time, Kenneth and Diana Rowntree had found a house at Acomb near Hexham in Northumberland, a remote base for an artist with national and international aspirations. This was different from living in Putney and if it gave Rowntree an opportunity to work out his own artistic innovations it was far from the rapid flow of the London art world. To sustain a profile would be challenging, though a successful solo exhibition was held at The New Art Centre in London in 1970. Commuting between London and Newcastle was a weekly necessity. Furthermore the Paris uprising of 1968 soon found an echo in London art schools, especially Hornsey College of Art. It also resounded through the Newcastle department, making its administration a cultural confrontation and even a physical danger.

In this demanding context it is surprising to discover Rowntree's involvement in February 1970 with the creation of the Serpentine Gallery in London, now such a vital centre of adventurous exhibition making. The Minister of Public Buildings and Works had agreed that the Arts Council would be responsible for administering the Kensington Tea House as an exhibition centre for four or five months in the summer, with special consideration for artists denied adequate opportunities for showing in London. Lawrence Gowing led the committee with Rowntree and Norbert Lynton. The Serpentine Gallery was chosen as its name. Initially the intention was to provide opportunities for former art students to exhibit.

Rowntree continued his study of verbal and visual imagery, various kinds of paint and the implications of collage construction.

One of Hamilton's extraordinary achievements at Newcastle had been to relocate part of the barn (or *Merzbarn*), in which the Dadaist Kurt Schwitters had made his last, large relief, from its rural location at Elterwater in the Lake District to the Hatton Gallery. Schwitters' use of extraneous objects, from string to a ceramic egg and pieces of watering can encouraged Rowntree's assemblages of materials. *Eyemouth Telegram*, for example, has only one touch of paint, and is otherwise made wholly from wooden boxes.

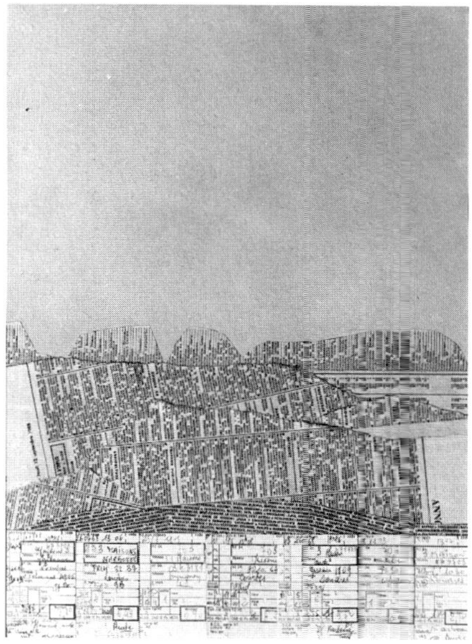

66 Foothills of the Pyrenees 1969
Acrylic paint and collage on board
50.8 x 38.1 cms (20 x 15 inches)

But Schwitters had also been a sound poet and a constructor of collages that frequently included words. This, too, encouraged Rowntree's visual/verbal experiments. The *Bürolandschaft* series of 1971 offered a new extension to the open-air still-life as he translated the term for open-plan office literally as 'office landscape'. As bureau in English can also mean a desk or cupboard, he added all of these aspects together for the series, varnishing wood panels for the office interior, but adding sky or other features to make it also a landscape in which a cupboard may seem enormous, like an arcaded building.

A variety of still-lifes followed, systematically combining new features with earlier formats. *Wooden Interior: London/Newcastle* (Fig.68) is the most elaborate relief. It is a shock to realise that this interior employs scarcely any paint. Tea chests and boxes here sum up the axis of so many of his journeys. The black lines of a Corbusier chair connect with a woven seat represented by drilled plywood.

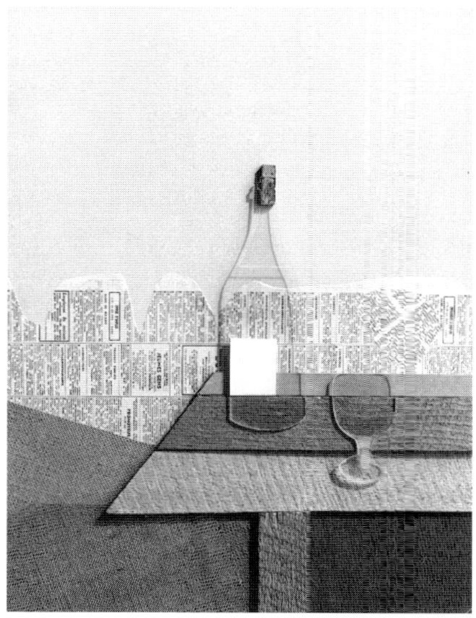

67 Bottle, Glass, Table: The Pyrenees 1970
Acrylic paint, wood, perspex and paper collage
61 x 49.6 cms (24 x 19.5 inches)

Rowntree's major exhibitions after the mid 1970s took place in the north of England with a few important displays elsewhere. There were two exhibitions in 1976, for example, one at the Gallery Colbert in Durham and a second at the Laing Art Gallery in Newcastle, opened by Lord Donaldson, Minister for the Arts.[87]

The Laing Art Gallery bought his imposing relief construction of the west front of Durham Cathedral, a return to the elevation format so familiar throughout his career. He added block lettering referring to the cathedral's history. *Epis*, for example, is a fragment of the Latin for bishop. He repeated the technique in *Souvenir of the Palace, Bishop Auckland* in 1974, referring to Bishop Pudsey as if in strange graffiti on the wall.[88]

Towards a Dynamic Landscape was the last theme of the series using lettered tea chests. Painted symbols and landscape references vie with

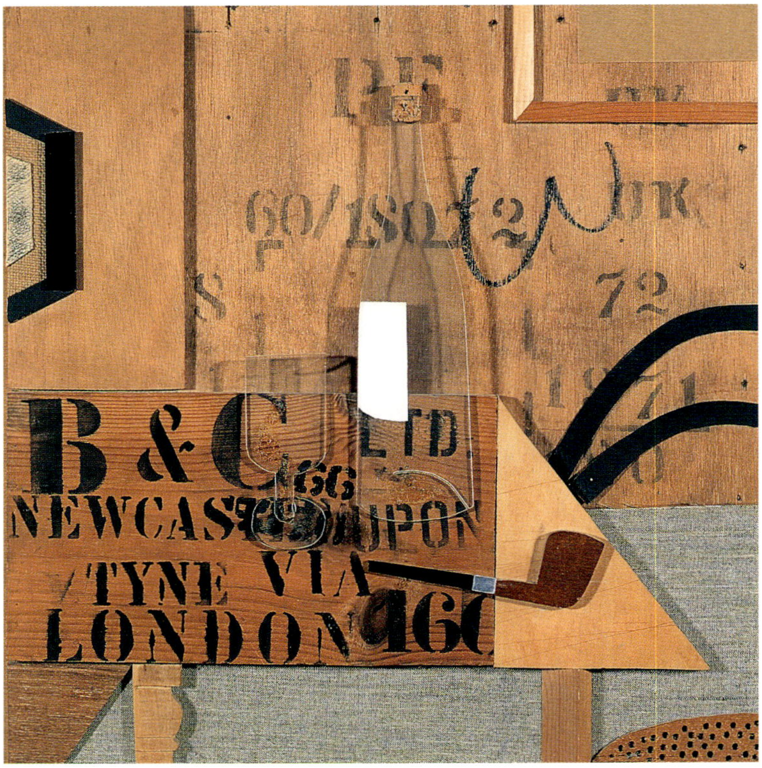

68 Wooden Interior: London/Newcastle 1974
Wood, fabric, cork and perspex on board
48.2 x 48.2 cms (19 x 19 inches)

the underlying rhythm of letters in a tumultuous juddering movement. The painted forms derive largely from the Venetian series paired here with new lettering motifs. These paintings were shown in an exhibition at York University in 1978.[89] A further exhibition followed at the Demarco Gallery, Edinburgh in 1979.

From the late 1970s onwards, Rowntree's sense of individual place grew ever stronger, rescued from his long experiment with Constructive art. If the later work is viewed as a contemplation of earlier themes, it is not surprising to see the return of topographical subjects. *Findochty*, of 1978, is a case in point with its houses along the harbour. The boats, lines and buoy are elements from years before that gather again into the recognisable portrait of a particular place.

There was also travel. When Diana Rowntree became involved in a committee on conservation and building in Jerusalem,[90] Kenneth went with her. A sequence of works came out of this which constructs through collage the drama of its clashing cultures, alphabets and architectural forms, its tawdrier aspects and its architectural magnificence. In *Jerusalem: Night Flight* he used metal foil stamped with grapes for the leaded steeples of churches. For the *Walls of*

Jerusalem he used Greek, Hebrew and Arabic newspapers to construct the walls and tickets to construct his flight.

Here was a painter with a wide range of approaches which he juxtaposed against each other in a creative interplay that could continue indefinitely, releasing new combinations, visual and verbal, in new visions of people, objects and places. The full range of his career was displayed at the Hatton Gallery on the occasion of his retirement in 1980. It provided a panorama of what Diana Rowntree has called, 'the baffling refusal of this artist to tread a rational path'.[91] Schwitters would have considered this high praise.

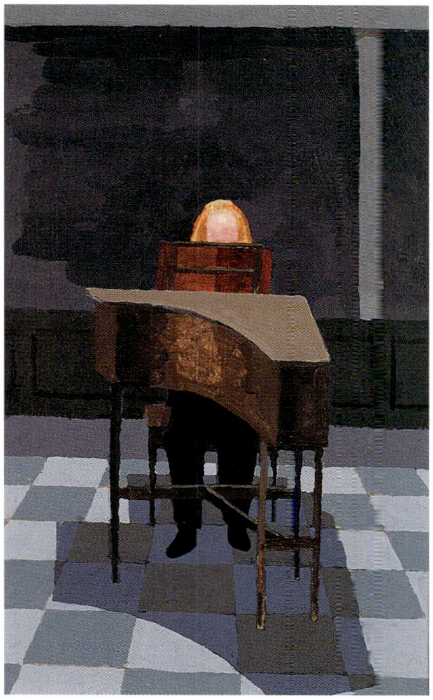

69 Portrait of Alan Fearon playing the Harpsichord 1981
Acrylic paint on board
39.4 x 28.6 cms (15.5 x 11.25 inches)
Collection Alan and Sarah Fearon

Retirement

In retirement, Rowntree found a new studio in Beaufront village, a few miles from his house in Northumberland. He was approaching the age at which an artist may be rediscovered by a younger audience. David Mellor's exhibition and book devoted to Recording Britain toured after opening at the Victoria and Albert Museum in 1988. It revealed again the fresh wartime watercolours and Rowntree's contribution to British painting in the 1940s. Michael Nixon organised a *Retrospective* in 1992 at the Davies Memorial Gallery in Newtown and at Oriel 31 in Welshpool, before touring it to Cardiff and to the Royal Festival Hall in London, close to the point where forty-one years earlier Rowntree had worked on his *Freedom* mural. Smaller exhibitions followed in Durham (1993), Kendal (1993) and Saffron Walden (1995).

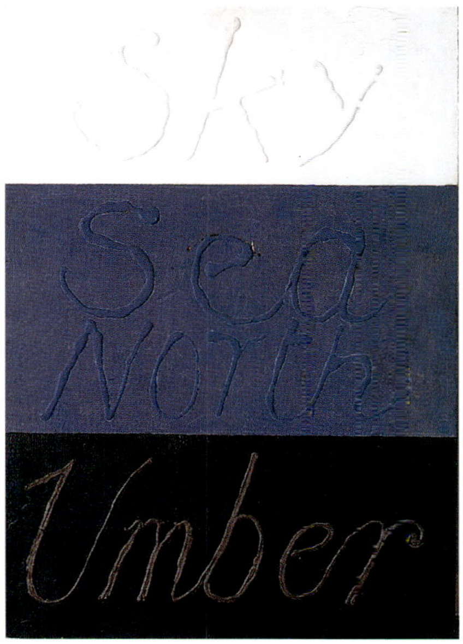

70 Sky Sea North Umber 1981
Acrylic paint on board
51 x 36 cms (20 x 14.25 inches)

Rowntree remained inventive. An exquisite *Portrait of Alan Fearon playing the Harpsichord* (Fig.69), a member of the Northern Sinfonia Orchestra and leader of its chorus, shows him seated at the harpsichord, his long hair recalling an eighteenth-century portrait. Rowntree's love of music met up with his verbal/visual analogies in the landscape collage *Monte Verdi* conjuring up musical and landscape references in the name. A similar use of relief lettering formed the succinct verbal/visual landscape *Sky Sea North Umber* (Fig.70), depicting a coastal scene through four words and four bands of colour (one of them raw umber), reusing the fragment *umber* with *north* to suggest Northumberland.

He continued to live in the village of Acomb until infirmity provoked a move to Corbridge in the Tyne Valley in 1988. Acomb, though elevated, is a dense group of houses and trees, of which he made several wooden

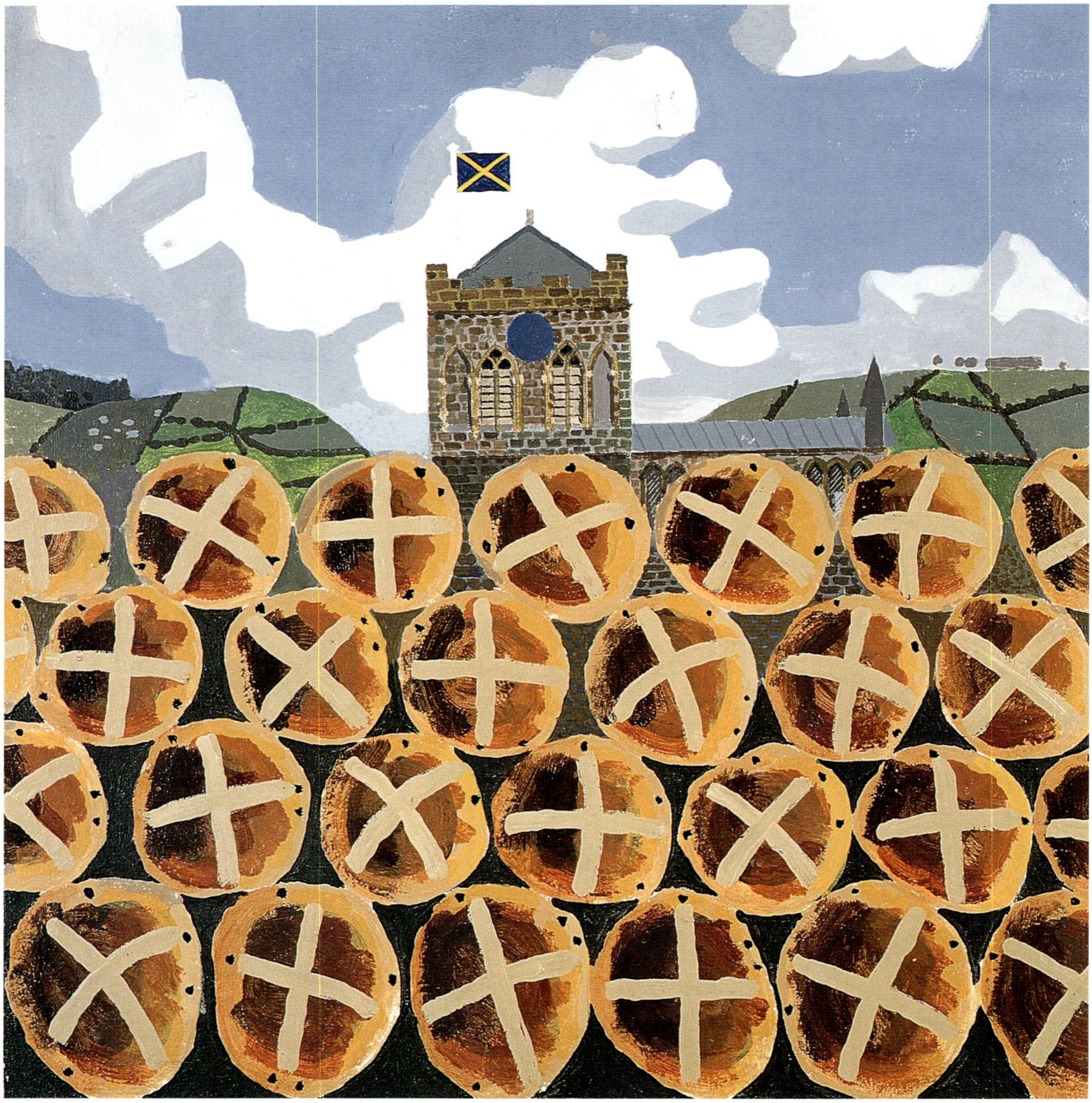

71 Easter Day, Hexham 1984
Acrylic paint on board
48.2 x 48.2 cms (19 x 19 inches)

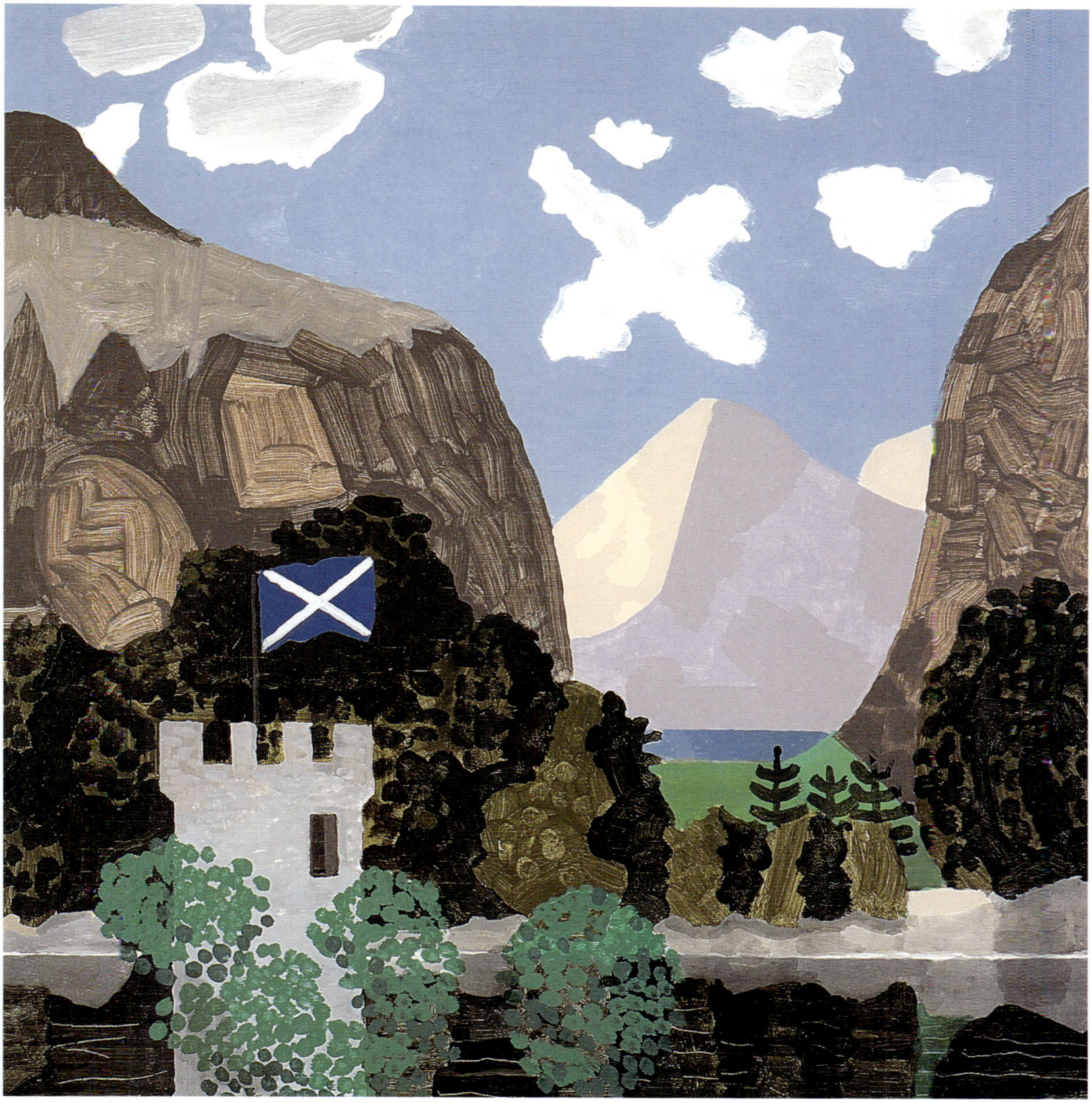

72 Windy Day in the Highlands 1984
Acrylic paint on board
59.7 x 59.7 cms (23.5 x 23.5 inches)

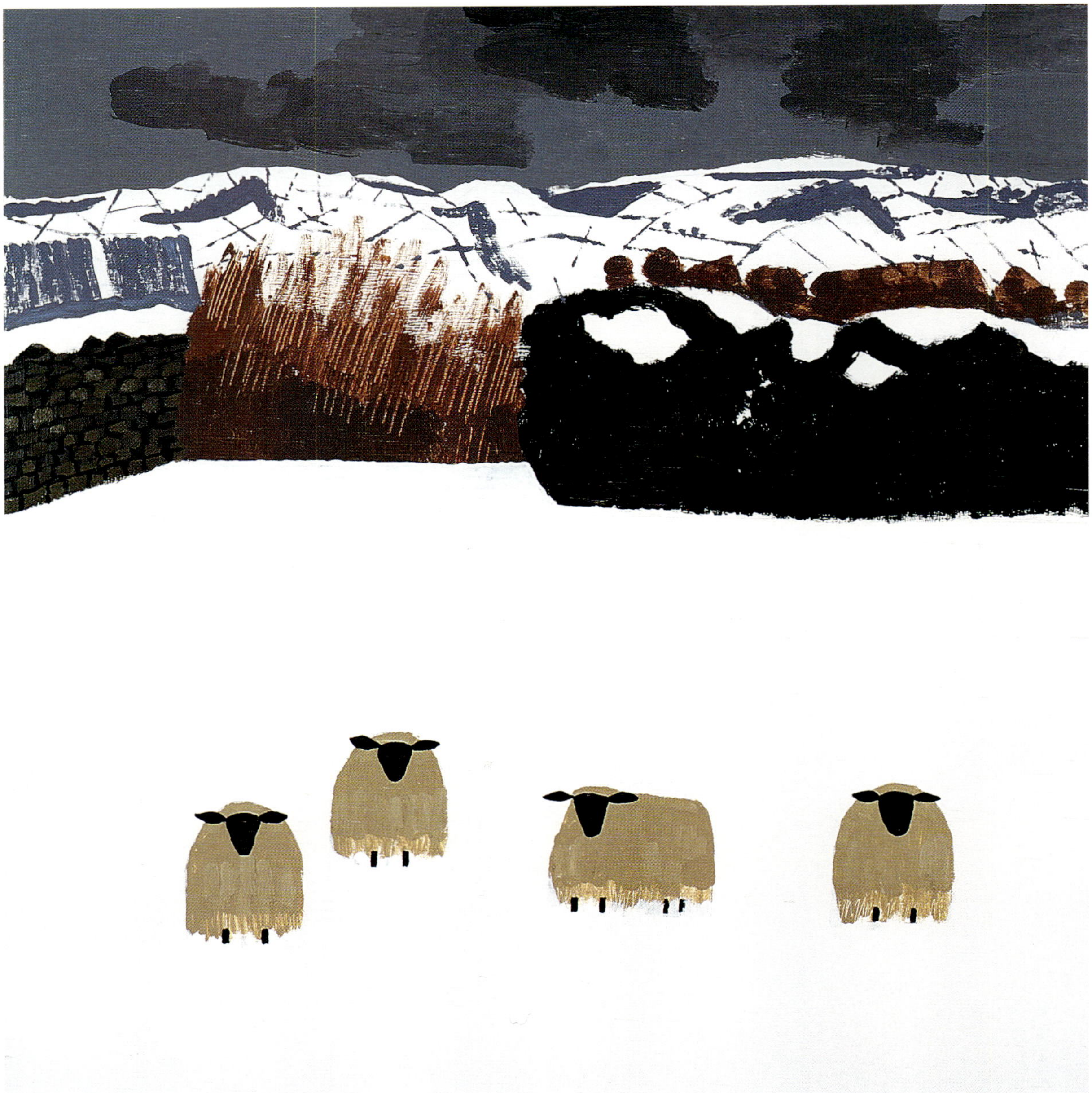

73 Tynedale, Winter 1984
Acrylic paint on board
61 x 61 cms (24 x 24 inches)

constructions representing the view from his house, drilling or scraping his plywood to make textures act like paint to differentiate trees, adding drawn lines to clarify the image. The effect remained painterly in every case, whether paint was employed or not.

Rowntree was interested in Hexham too. *Easter Day, Hexham* (Fig.71) of 1984 presents a preposterous profusion of hot cross buns, their aroma pervading the Abbey precincts. It is a celebration of Easter's popularity, a visual delight in the crosses that refer to it, and pleasure in the peculiarity of the bun as a cultural phenomenon, as well as a reminder of the church as history, geography and identity.

Windy Day in the Highlands (Fig.72), 1984, is one of the long series of elaborate and decorative later landscapes, convincing in their light and character despite the toy-like simplicity of forms which comprise them. *Tynedale, Winter* (Fig.73) is another example of this achievement. Construction has, on the whole, given way once more to the recognisable image (Fig.74). In his screenprint *Verlaine* (Fig.78), with the French poet's '*sanglots longs/des violons/de l'automne*', there is a fusion of poetic, musical and visual references that recalls the enthusiasms of his *Homage to French Culture in the Nineteenth Century*, painted forty-six years earlier.

Despite a productive visit to Australia in 1984, Rowntree gradually attuned his visual acuity and intelligence to more local subjects in a series of paintings that lost none of the flair and freshness of earlier works. *Naming of Parts* (Fig.75), for example, shows Acomb Village across his garden, each part labelled with its name.

In 1990, Rowntree suffered a detached retina which was not effectively cured by an operation that terrified him. Vision remained good in the other eye, but he was afraid the surgeon would operate on the wrong eye. He wanted to write *This Eye* with an arrow on his cheek, a grimmer naming of the parts. But it did not prevent a whole sequence of late still-lifes, some of which contained extraordinary new ideas.

Byzantine Teapot (Fig.77), painted in 1989–90, is one of the last open-air landscapes. The landscape is spacious, colourful and easy to read. The teapot is incorporated into the landscape with no table top to support it. By adding to the dome of its lid a small white cross, Rowntree has once more sprung a metaphor, transforming the teapot into a Greek church. Conversely, the handle and spout reassert the image of the teapot to reveal the architectural qualities of ordinary kitchenware. Its shaded side is Greek newsprint. The open-air still-life has taken on new ambiguities.

There is in this painting the wit that persisted throughout his life, finding comparisons, reversals, metaphors and insights that were startling and astute in imagery, words and in his vision of the world. He was as adept in French too, creating double meanings as surprising as a *Byzantine Teapot*. He once described a student's feint drawing of a duck as a 'mallard imaginaire', and complained about a Civic Centre's carillon as those 'damn bells sans merci'.

Kenneth Rowntree died on 21 February 1997.

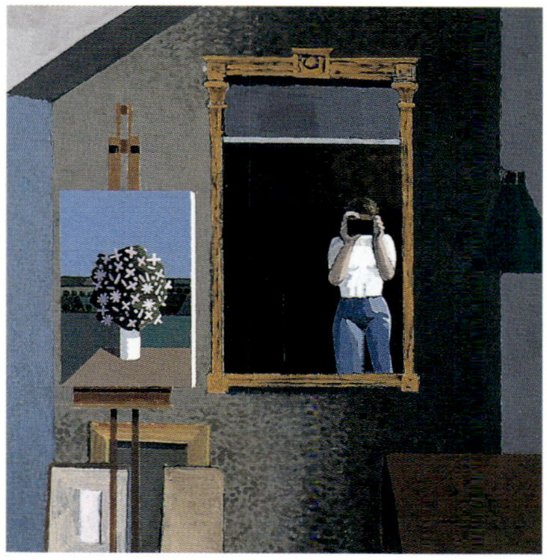

74 The Photographer in the Studio 1983
Acrylic paint on board
82 x 82 cms (32.5 x 32.5 inches)

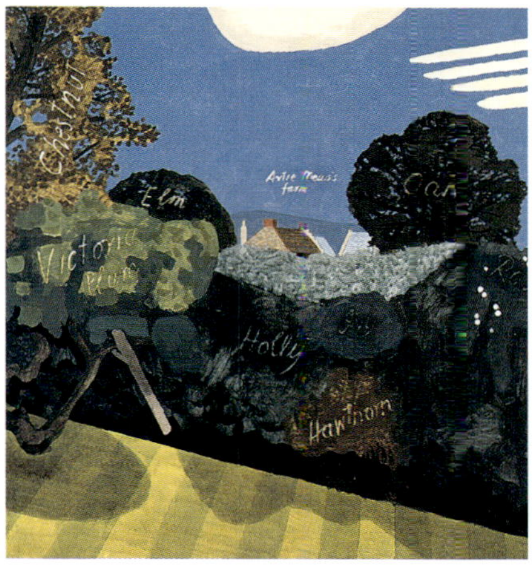

75 Naming of Parts 1987
Acrylic paint on board
60.5 x 60.5 cms (23.75 x 23.75 inches)

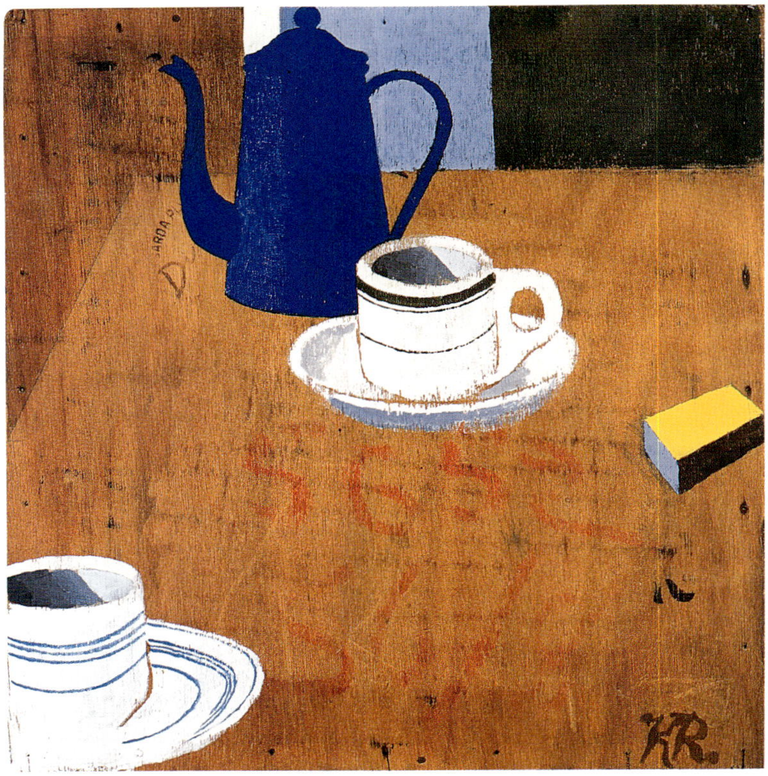

76 The Blue Coffee Pot 1988
Acrylic paint on board
48.3 x 48.3 cms (19 x 19 inches)
Collection Mrs Humphrey Odd

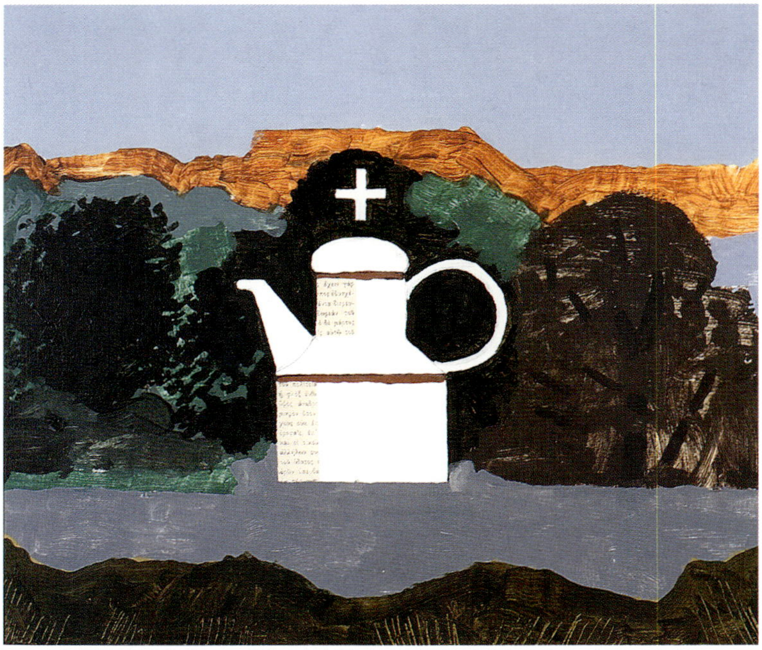

77 Byzantine Teapot 1990
Acrylic paint on board
50.8 x 58.5 cms (20 x 23 inches)

Endnotes

1 Anonymous, *Anecdotes of the Quakers, Instructive and Amusing, of their Shrewdness, Wit, Disinterestedness, Benevolence, and Moral Heroism*, Nottingham, no date, p.9.

2 Paul Nash was officially a visiting lecturer but, according to Diana Rowntree, he was never seen.

3 Rutherston exhibited regularly with the New English Art Club between 1900 and 1940. He was made an Associate of the Royal Watercolour Society (ARWS) in 1934.

4 Rowntree was also taught by the painter and graphic artist Eric Ravilious at Oxford. Later they became close friends.

5 The painting was made in 1938 for John (Jack) and Yvonne Liddicott for their new home in Scarborough, Yorkshire. The doors were to divide off the dining room from the hall and the triptych was painted directly onto them for an agreed price of £5. Lamartine's Lac du Bourget appears at the left. The cliffs of Normandy fill the centre area before which appear the figure of Courbet and a girl derived from a group portrait by Degas. Paris harbours artists and writers at the right.

6 These included *Allotments at Gisors* 1936, *Gisors* 1938, *Washstand at Gisors* 1939, *From a café window Gisors* 1939, and *Tide Signals, Fécamp* 1939.

7 Paul Nash, for example, exploited these possibilities and became one of the most influential of the British artists who responded to Surrealist ideas.

8 Harries, M. & Harries, S., *The War Artists*, London, 1983, p.156ff. Clark had little belief in the Munich agreement and had already begun to close the National Gallery section by section. See Clark, K., *Another Part of the Wood: A Self Portrait*, London, 1974.

9 Harries, M. & Harries, S., 1983, p.156.

10 Diana Rowntree's memory of Lawn Road Flats is given in Pritchard, J., *View from a Long Chair*, introduction by Fiona McCarthy, London, 1984, pp.96–7.

11 For example, the catalogue of Rowntree's exhibition at the Leicester Galleries, London, in 1946 listed a painting called *Cavendish Road, Clare, Suffolk* and dated 1938.

12 From a chronological note by Diana Rowntree, typescript, 2000.

13 Letter of 3 October 1939 from Kenneth Clark to Lambert Wolf at the Ministry of Labour, cited in Mellor, D., Saunders, G. & Wright, P., *Recording Britain: A Pictorial Doomsday of Pre-War Britain*, London, 1990. See also Clark, K., *The Other Half: A Self Portrait*, London, 1977.

14 Mellor et al., 1990, p.17.

15 Mellor et al.,1990, p.7.

16 Rowntree also made some of favourite places, for example, *The Bellringers' Chamber, Saints Peter and Paul's Church, Clare* and *Interior of the Baptist Chapel, Clare*, both now in the Victoria and Albert Museum (E.2159–1949 and E.2160–1949 respectively).

17 Mellor et al., 1990, pp.9–10; Garlake, M., *New Art, New World: British Art in postwar Society*, London and New Haven, 1998, p.95, notes that 'Kenneth Rowntree, much praised by contemporary writers, was one of the very few artists to extend the conventions of topographic watercolour, introducing an element of modernising *faux naïveté* into his *Underbank farm, Woodlands, Ashdale, Derbyshire* (1940) with its mauve roofs and purple highlights.'

18 Mellor et al., 1990, p.10. The Town and Country Planning Act was not passed until 1947, so Clark's anxieties about development were justified and were shared by many in the aftermath of run-away suburban development in the inter-war years.

19 A comparable irony on the theme of submersion probably informed Rowntree's *The Bathroom, Ashopton Inn, Derbyshire* (1940) now in the Victoria and Albert Museum (E.1267–1949).

20 This recalls Paul Nash's evocations of strange places and ancient times.

21 Rowntree's other Ashopton watercolours include *Ashopton from the New Road* (now in the Victoria and Albert Museum, E.1260–1949), *Cox's farm and white House* (E.1261–1949), *Bridge at Cox's farm* (E.1262–1949), *Ashopton Inn showing Bamford Edge* (E.1263–1949), *Ashopton Inn, Main Doorway* (E.1264–1949), *The Ladybower Inn* (E.1268–1949), *The Old Toll Bar House* (E.1269–1949), and also *The Crescent Buxton* (E.1271–1949), *Grainfoot farm, Derwentdale* (E.1272–1949), and *Bridge End farm, Derwent village* (E.1273–1949).

22 The catalogue of Rowntree's exhibition at the Leicester Galleries, London, in 1946 listed a painting of *Eric and Thirzah Ravilious* made in 1941.

23 Rowntree executed twelve watercolours of Essex for Recording Britain now in the Victoria and Albert Museum (E.1407–1949 to E.1418–1949) including subjects in Barnston, Finchingfield, Great Bardfield, Lindsell, and Tilty.

24 The architectural historian (Sir) Nikolaus Pevsner was helpful to Rowntree in Essex where he lived. Pevsner wrote on the Black Chapel, North End, in his early volume on Essex in the *Buildings of England* series, describing it as 'a rare, entirely timber-framed ecclesiastical building', *Essex*, London, 1954, p.280.

25 Rowntree executed twelve watercolours of Yorkshire for Recording Britain, now in the Victoria and Albert Museum (E.2537–1949 to E.2592–1949) including subjects in Beverley, Cranthorne, Flamborough, Guisborough, Ryedale, Rievaulx, Scarborough, Sheriff Hutton and York.

26 Rowntree also made eight watercolours in Bedfordshire, now in the Victoria and Albert Museum (E.1070–1949 to E.1077–1949) including subjects in Ampthill, Dunstable and Toternhoe.

27 Another repeated motif was gravestones, of which Rowntree made numerous drawings in 1943. He made eight watercolours of Caernarvonshire for Recording Britain, now in the Victoria and Albert Museum (E.2418–1949 to E.2426–1949).

28 CEMA was the Council for the Encouragement of Music and Arts, which after the war formed a basis for the Arts Council.

29 The critic Eric Newton reviewed the scheme in *The Listener*, 2 July 1942, p.7.

30 His earliest mural was in Scarborough Library. It convinced the Liddicotts of Rowntree's ability to paint their screen. It was apparently painted out in the 1950s.

31 Letter of 14 November 1944 from Kenneth Clark to Kenneth Rowntree, written from the National Gallery. Rowntree was to paint one London subject for Recording Britain, entitled *The Pantechnicon, Motcomb Street, SW1*, now in the Victoria and Albert Museum (E.1862–1949).

32 According to the catalogue of Rowntree's exhibition at the Leicester Galleries, London, in 1946 other paintings dating from 1944 included *Pub at Llangollen*, *Girl doing her Hair* and *Three Cows*.

33 Letter of 14 November 1944 from Kenneth Clark to Kenneth Rowntree.

34 The catalogue of Rowntree's exhibition at the Leicester Galleries, London, in 1946 listed the following works dating from 1942: *Empty House*, *Portrait of Mr Davey, Painter and Decorator*, and *Adam Rowntree*. Works from 1943 included *Road Sign and Water pump*, *Bather in a Wood*, and *The Shunter*.

35 Recording Britain was wound up in 1946, and published as *Recording Britain*, Oxford University Press in 1946, in four volumes.

36 The Tate Gallery has dated the painting to 1952 but it was illustrated in *The Studio*, February 1947, with a Leicester Galleries credit line. It was also exhibited in Oxford in 1950.

37 The catalogue of Rowntree's exhibition at the Leicester Galleries, London, in 1946 included *The Sadler's Shop at Clare*, *Near the station, Dunmow*, *Crescent Gardens, Scarborough*, *Lindsell landscape*, *Bardfield Gardens* and *the Footbridge and Railway Yard, Clare*.

38 *1946 Spring Contemporaries*, exh.cat., City of Leicester Art Gallery, 16 February–31 March 1946, p.2.

39 *1946 Spring Contemporaries*, p.2. Rowntree exhibited *Level Crossing, Evening*, watercolour, 50.8 x 25.4 cm (20 x 10 in) and *Mlle Manicette Carrière*, oil, 53.3 x 71.1 cm (21 x 28 in).

40 See Spalding, F., *British Art since 1900*, London, 1989, p.137.

41 Rowntree, K., *A Prospect of Wales*, Harmondsworth, 1948. Diana Rowntree recalls that 'the painter is acknowledged before the writer because KR was originally to illustrate a book to be written by Clough William-Ellis. However when Clough saw the illustrations which became so popular in the *Prospect of Wales* he did not care for KR's sardonic approach – showing barbed-wire fences and humble artisans' terraces .... He declined to write the text, and Gwyn Jones took it over.'

42 *A Prospect of Wales: twenty-one watercolour drawings of Wales by Kenneth Rowntree*, exh.cat., 1949, p.2.

43 *Eric Ravilious Memorial Exhibition*, exh.cat., Tower Art Gallery, Eastbourne and Brighton Art Gallery, 1948, p.5.

44 Pasmore, V., *Abstract Art: Comments by Some Artists and Critics*, London, 1949.

45 Pasmore was impressed by Charles Biederman's *Art as the Evolution of Visual Knowledge*, Minnesota, 1948, with its theories of creative construction and illustrations of works by Mondrian, Van Doesburg, Van Tongerloo and by Biederman himself.

46 *Watercolours by Kenneth Rowntree*, exh.cat., Leicester Galleries, London, 1950, p.2.

47 *The South Bank Exhibition, London, 1951. Festival of Britain. A Guide to the Story it Tells*, HMSO, London, 1951, p.67.

48 *The South Bank Exhibition*, 1951, p.68.

49 Rowntree worked closer to his Recording Britain style on covers for a series of guides, *Around Britain*, published by Collins and distributed at the Festival of Britain. Rowntree illustrated no.7, *North Wales and the Marches*, as well no.10, *The Lakes to Tyneside*.

50 He was also exhibiting with the activist group, *Artists for Peace*, who held exhibitions at the Royal Hotel, Woburn Place, London, in 1951–3. Other exhibitors included Pasmore, Minton, Ruskin Spear, and in 1952 Léger, Picasso, Lurçat and Gromaire.

51 Letter of 25 March 1953 from A. W. Cunliffe at Lambeth Bridge House, to Kenneth Rowntree.

52 *The Coronation of Her Majesty Queen Elizabeth II: Paintings and Drawings*, exh.cat., Ministry of Works, London, 1953.

53 Letter of 9 June 1954. Rowntree's other ocean-going murals were made for RMS *Orcades* (before 1951) and RMS *Orsova* of the Orient Line.

54 Cat.nos 78 & 86.

55 Rowntree, D., 'Oxford college barges: their history and decay, and their successors the boathouses', *Architectural Review*, 1956, nos 7–12, pp.37–42.

56 Rowntree, D., 1956, p.37.

57 Rowntree, D., 1956, p.38.

58 Rowntree, D., 1956, p.38.

59 This was cited in the exhibition catalogue, *The Oxford Barges. Kenneth Rowntree*, Keble College, Oxford, in association with the Bear Lane Gallery, Oxford, 1959.

60 *The Oxford Barges. Kenneth Rowntree*, 1959.

61 Several sources refer to a mural at the Brussels World Fair of 1958 but no documentation or evidence for it has materialised. It is possible that the commission itself never materialised. Works by Rowntree's friends Edward Bawden and Peggy Angus were exhibited there.

62 Letter of 8 July 1958 from Robin Darwin, Rector of the Royal College of Art, to Kenneth Rowntree.

63 Friendly, R., 'Painter's delight: Britisher loves our cemeteries', *New Orleans States and New Orleans Item*, 8 April 1959.

64 Watercolours exhibited in *Kenneth Rowntree* at the Zwemmer Gallery, London, 1962, included *Inn Yard, Taos*; *Sun Going Down, New Mexico*; *Indian Fence, Taos*; *Crosses, New Mexico*, and *Landscape, New Mexico*.

65 Watercolours exhibited in *Kenneth Rowntree* at the Zwemmer Gallery, London, 1962, included *Nantucket I*; *Nantucket II*; *Lighthouse Nantucket (Sankaty Head)*; *Into the Sun, Nantucket* and *Roofs, Nantucket*.

66 Friendly, 1959.

67 *Paintings, Drawings and Lithographs by Past and Present Masters, Teachers and Students. The Ruskin School of Drawing and Fine Art, Oxford*, June–July 1959 (Typescript in the Ashmolean Museum Library, Oxford).

68 Biederman, 1948, p.522.

69 Discussed in Bowness, A., 'The paintings and constructions of Victor Pasmore', *Burlington Magazine*, May 1960, pp.198–205. This reference p.202.

70 Thompson, D. W., *Growth and Form*, Cambridge, 1948.

71 Alloway, L., 'Victor Pasmore makes a relief', *Art News*, Summer 1956.

72 *An Exhibit 2, with Victor*, exh.cat., Hatton Gallery, University of Durham at Newcastle, 1959.

73 *The Developing Process*, exh.cat., Hatton Gallery, University of Durham at Newcastle and ICA, London, 1959.

74 *The Developing Process*, 1959, p.1.

75 See *The Developing Process*, 1959, p.1.

76 *The Developing Process*, 1959, p.2.

77 *The Developing Process*, 1959, p.3.

78 *The Developing Process*, 1959, p.19.

79 *Victor Pasmore*, exh.cat., Hatton Gallery, University of Durham at Newcastle, May 1960. Diana Rowntree maintains that Kenneth Rowntree as professor 'was a supporter and enabler to staff and students. Pasmore's recognition of this was to tell Kenneth to choose any Pasmore that he liked as a present.' (note to the author, August 2001)

80 *Paintings from the Estorick Collection*, Hatton Gallery, University of Durham at Newcastle, 1960.

81 The forms are reminiscent of the paintings of the Russian artist Malevich.

82 Rowntree made at least thirteen variations on this theme.

83 Zwemmer was selling the watercolours for £45 at this time. Overall sales were an impressive £872. Expenses including commission to the Gallery (33 per cent), framing, installation and private view costs reduced the income to £485, still a sign of success. In addition, an article on Rowntree appeared in the Anglo-American periodical, *The Painter and Sculptor*, vol.5, no.1, Summer 1962.

84 A comparable collage-painting exists called *Connemara Window*, 1963, which also features window motif, mug, hillside and vigorous assemblage effects.

85 Hamilton, R., *Diagram and 'The Green Book', The Bride Stripped Bare by Her Bachelors, Even*, London, 1960.

86 Rowntree painted a *Homage to Apollinaire* in 1979.

87 *Kenneth Rowntree: Paintings, Drawings and Collages*, exh.cat., Laing Art Gallery, Newcastle, 1976.

88 Kenneth Rowntree also produced the comparable *West Front, Durham*, 1976, screenprint on paper, 48.3 x 48.8 cm (19 x 19.25 in), Tate Gallery, London (P02836).

89 *Kenneth Rowntree: Paintings*, Heslington Hall, University of York, 20 February–17 March 1978. In addition to tea chests, Rowntree used boards that friends had found on beaches.

90 Diana Rowntree recently described the Jerusalem Committee as 'a pressure group assembled from a wide range of nationalities to add respectability to the Israelis' attempt to resist the partition of Jerusalem.'

91 Diana Rowntree, chronological note, typescript, 2000.

Chronology
by Diana Rowntree

The chapters of Kenneth's life seem to have been its locations.

Yorkshire 1915–32
He was born into a Quaker family in Scarborough. His father, Howard, managed his family's department store with considerable flair. His mother, Nora Priestman, was a Bradford Quaker whose family included the nineteenth-century radical MP John Bright and Bertram Priestman RA. Nora, a violinist, was trained at the Royal College of Music. His father had cleverly discovered the Downs School, Herefordshire, whose art master, Maurice Feild recognised his ability, and encouraged it, as he did Lawrence Gowing's. Kenneth Rowntree followed his brothers to Bootham School, York, where he greatly enjoyed the arts subjects, especially French, and the freedom to explore the city, its markets and pork pies. Poor mathematics debarred him from the sixth form. He went to the Ruskin Drawing School, Oxford, which was intended to prepare him for the Slade.

Oxford 1932–4
1932 The Ruskin Drawing School was then a very small art school. A few students bent on becoming professional artists were outnumbered by undergraduates who snatched what time they could in the Ruskin studio. The principal, Albert Rutherston, was a delightful man who spoiled the serious students. He thought Humphrey Waterfield and Kenneth Rowntree the most promising.

Much of the teaching was done by visiting artists. Kenneth looked forward to Paul Nash's visit, but Nash did not materialise. One regular was Barnett Freedman – famous for telling a dim girl 'if you crossed the road with as much intelligence as you did this drawing you'd be RUN OVER.' Kenneth admired the work of a gentler teacher, Eric Ravilious, who became our friend.

1933 Kenneth won the Life Drawing Prize

1934 Kenneth won the Life Painting Prize. I joined the Ruskin School's first year class in architecture.

London 1935–41
Settled in Windmill Street, off Tottenham Court Road. Kenneth followed the Ruskin School's relaxed routine which had not toughened him enough to weather the taxing climate at the Slade. Slade students, confronted by the powerful personalities and highly conflicting views of the teaching staff, had to discover their own style and fight their corner. Kenneth preferred to arrange his ideas in his own studio, and gradually dropped out of the Slade, always heeding Barnett Freedman's warning, that if artists did not spend their time at the easel they would miss the rare moments of inspiration when they came.

During the vacations his father's civic connections brought Kenneth jobs – murals in the Children's Library in Scarborough, and one on a folding screen for a chemistry master and his French wife. He responded to the French connection with his most subtle work to date, which has been superbly preserved.

He got to know the world of his London contemporaries, joined the New English Art Club and its like, and began to sell work at Wildenstein's, Zwemmer's and the Leicester Galleries. He must also have served on committees, as he learned to despise them wholeheartedly.

1939 I qualified as an architect in the summer. We were considering marriage when war broke out in September. Fearing annihilation, we opted for a Registrar's office, and enjoyed a miniscule reception on the eating area at Lawn Road Flats, Hampstead.

After months as guests or lodgers with friends, a kindly bomb regained us entry into Lawn Road, where we found the concrete world as stimulating as we had imagined (and drawn) it.

But ten months later the onset of a baby set us house hunting in 'the country' and the Raviliouses helped us to find a handsome draughty house in Great Bardfield where we lived for a year.

Essex 1941–9

As a conscientious objector Kenneth could not become an official war artist, but the Recording Britain scheme miraculously employed him. He chose to record Yorkshire, his birthplace, Essex, where he lived, Derbyshire, where an area to be flooded by a new reservoir needed recording, and Wales, where he illustrated the King Penguin book *A Prospect of Wales*.

1942 Our son Adam was born on 13 March.

A mural for Acton's British Restaurant changed the scale of Kenneth's activities.

1943 We moved a few miles from Great Bardfield to 'Simpkins' in the village of Lindsell on the road to Dunmow.

1947 On 12 March, in that bleak winter our daughter Sasha was born.

1949–50 Kenneth painted a mural for the Barclay School, Stevenage, a large comprehensive that has looked after it well.

Before Kenneth became so itinerant we had moved to a lonely farmhouse. Two years later the closure of our village school caused us reluctantly to send Adam to board at a small school in Aldeburgh. Robin Darwin was our saviour, offering Kenneth charge of mural painting at the Royal College of Art.

London 1950–70

We found a house on the Thames, upstream of Putney Bridge, and turned the attic into a studio. Its comfort permanently slowed Kenneth's working speed from the swift tempo demanded by one-day forays into distant landscapes.

At the end of the school year Adam started at a local day school, run by the Froebel Institute, and when Sasha joined him there, I started freelancing, later becoming Architecture correspondent at *The Guardian*.

1950 A one-man exhibition opened at the Leicester Galleries. Hugh Casson, Professor of Interior Design at the Royal College of Art, commissioned a mural for the Lion and Unicorn Pavilion at the forthcoming Festival of Britain.

1953 When the coronation came Kenneth was given a free brief and chose to paint the carting away of horse shit after the procession had passed down the Mall. Casson also included two Rowntree paintings in his scheme for the Queen's private apartments.

1958 Kenneth's Royal College contract ended. With Adam now at Bootham School, York, our regular income needed to be speedily replaced. Rowntree had his admirers but was never trendy, which was bad news when looking for a prestigious job in London. With Darwin's backing he was offered the Chair, vacated by Lawrence Gowing, at Durham University's Fine Art Department based in Newcastle. Victor Pasmore and Richard Hamilton were on the staff and the atmosphere was exhilarating. Kenneth had taken up a bursary from the Ford Foundation, so could not start work in Newcastle for a term.

Newcastle 1959–80

1959 He returned from the United States with a set of watercolours that later sold well at the Zwemmer Gallery (1962), and he took up the Chair of Fine Art at Newcastle.

1963 Newcastle University split off from Durham University and exhilaration became the mood of the whole campus.

The new professor enjoyed his role, and related to the students with wit and an ability to surprise. He was less popular with the Administration Department.

Unfortunately this was also the year that Zwemmer closed his gallery, leaving Rowntree, who was then learning the many facets of his job, without an agent. He had no energy left to face attempting to find a dealer who appreciated his abilities as Zwemmer had done. His professional career suffered accordingly.

We were house-hunting in a county of few houses, spending alternate weekends in Newcastle and London. We lived on this axis until Sasha graduated as a typographer and left home to live with Esmond Devas, son of the painter Anthony Devas. Then we moved into a beautiful square stone house that we had honed into the first 'machine for living in' we had really enjoyed since Lawn Road days.

1976 He had a one-man exhibition at the Colbert Gallery, Durham, which belonged to Winston Barnett, and in December of that year the Director of Newcastle's Laing Art Gallery invited him to be the first artist to show in the Laing's new gallery. Kenneth hung the exhibition himself, and it was opened by Lord Donaldson, Minister for the Arts. Tyne and Wear Museums bought the wood construction *West Front Durham* for the permanent collection.

1978 A one-man exhibition was held at York University.

1979 A one-man exhibition followed at the Demarco Gallery in Edinburgh. Demarco had long appreciated Kenneth's work.

Northumberland 1980–97

1980 On his retirement the retrospective in the Hatton Gallery at Newcastle University was, with 191 works, his largest exhibition. It was well attended and greatly enhanced his reputation.

Kenneth had been looking forward to painting full time, and left the busy, populous life of responsibility with no worry or nostalgia. He simply looked round for a studio and found one within 200 yards of his house. Later he moved to the hind's cottage of a farm, where the ground floor room was the studio and the first floor became a well-lit picture gallery. This studio was the deciding factor between spending our old age in the Tyne valley or moving southwards to lighter skies.

1988 We moved to Corbridge. Soon after this a detached retina left Kenneth's right eye virtually useless, but we were then amazed to see him produce a faultless copy of the painting *Girl in Three Parts*.

The same year David Mellor's *Recording Britain* touring exhibition opened at the Victoria and Albert Museum. The accompanying book by Mellor, Gill Saunders and Patrick Wright had truer colour than the wartime publication of *Recording Britain*, and the authors' high regard for Rowntree's work was echoed by the national newspapers.

1991 August. His last visit to France.

1992 A one-man exhibition at the Davies Gallery, Newtown, in mid-Wales, went on to South Wales and to the Royal Festival Hall, London.

1993 A retrospective exhibition at the Durham Light Infantry Gallery was followed by one at Kendal.

1995 Rowntree's last retrospective was at the Fry Public Art Gallery, Saffron Walden, a gallery set up to celebrate 'the Bardfield Artists', now rechristened 'the North West Essex Artists'.

That autumn the electrical equipment at the studio failed and Kenneth retired to a small room at home in Corbridge to paint and look at the Tyne. He still enjoyed family life and being driven about the countryside.

1997 Most of all he enjoyed surprising his friends with his unique wit, which caused hilarity almost until the day he died on 21 February.

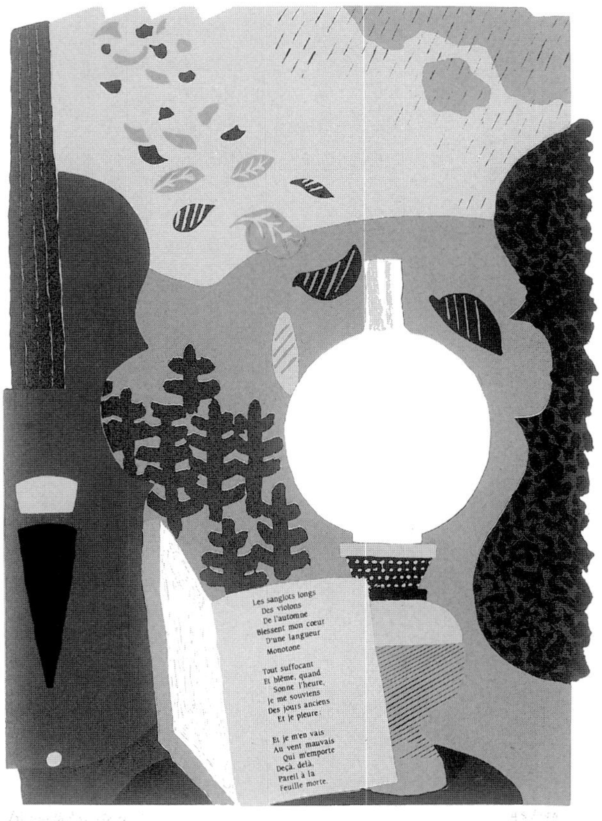

78 Verlaine 1984
Screenprint on paper
54.1 x 40.4 cms (21.25 x 17.25 inches)
The Tate Gallery, London (T02837)
Presented by the artist 1985

Index of Works